America's Favorites, Naturally

Victoria P. Cavalier

Melius & Peterson Publishing Corporation

Aberdeen, South Dakota

First Edition

Copyright © 1987 by Victoria P. Cavalier

Published in the United States by Melius & Peterson Publishing Corporation, Aberdeen, South Dakota 57401.

Bernie Seward/Artisan Photography *Photography and Photo Composition*
Kitchen Connection, Aberdeen *Tableware and Glassware* (*photos*)
Victoria P. Cavalier *Illustrations*

Library of Congress Cataloging-in-Publication Data

Cavalier, Victoria, 1952–
  America's favorites, naturally.

  Bibliography: p.
  Includes index.
  1. Cookery (Natural foods)   I. Title.
TX741.C38 1986   641.5'637   86–50166
ISBN 0–9610130–6–0
ISBN 0–9610130–5–2 (pbk.)

cover photo: Fresh Strawberry Cheesecake

DEDICATION

This book is dedicated to my children with all my love.

I'd like to thank my parents, Ralph and Jean Peterson, for their unconditional love and for instilling in me an appreciation for fine food. I was very fortunate to grow up in a home with two excellent cooks. Anna and Tom Cavalier also deserve a great deal of credit for their culinary guidance and experience. Thank you Bernie Seward for your time, talent, patience and wisdom.

Ian, thank you for being such an agreeable taste-tester, and Sierra thank you for inspiring many recipe adaptations in order to meet your finicky standards. I appreciate my children's patience and encouragement while I worked on this book. To Ken, my best friend, thank you for believing in me and for your loyal support.

TABLE OF CONTENTS

Introduction   ix

CHAPTER 1   Making a Change for the Better   1
Grains and Flours   4
Sweeteners   4
Protein Sources   5
Fruits and Vegetables   5
Cooking Oils   5
Condiments and Baking Needs   6
Cookware and Appliances   6

CHAPTER 2   Breads   7
Whole Wheat Bread   11
Cinnamon Raisin Bread   12
Cinnamon Raisin Caramel Rolls   12
Whole Wheat Rolls   13
Onion Bread   13
Pumpernickel Bread   13
English Muffins   14
Cinnamon Raisin English Muffins   14
Whole Wheat Egg Bagels   15
Cinnamon Raisin Whole Wheat Egg Bagels   15
Onion Whole Wheat Egg Bagels   15
Pita Bread   16
Boston Brown Bread   16
Pumpkin Bread   17
Corn Bread   17
Gingerbread   18
Carrot Coconut Bread   18
Banana Bread   19
Banana Nut Muffins   20
Bran Muffins   20
Biscuits   20
Crêpes   21
Tortillas   21
Whole Wheat Noodles†   22
Basic Pie Crust   22
Tomato Rye Pie Crust   23
Coconut Pie Crust†   23

CHAPTER 3   Breakfasts   25
Omelet   28
Cheese Omelet   28
Fruit Omelet   28
Scrambled Eggs   29
French Toast†   30
Pancakes   30
Orange Coconut Coffee Cake   31
Blintzes   32
Instant Blintz†   32
Cinnamon Raisin Oatmeal   33
Fruit and Nut Granola†   33
Maple Granola†   34
Peanut Butter Granola†   34
Carob-Peanut Butter Granola†   35
Strawberry Coconut Granola†   35
Broiled Grapefruit†   35
Baked Apples†   36

† indicates the recipe is either salt free or has no added salt.

Winter Fruit Salad†   37
Summer Fruit Salad†   37
Sunny Fruit Compote†   38
Spicy Fruit Compote†   38
Yogurt†   39
Kibbutz Breakfast†   39
Toddler Breakfasts†   40

CHAPTER 4   Soups, Vegetables and Condiments   41
Turkey Vegetable Soup   44
Chili   45
Chicken Noodle Soup   46
Bean Soup   47
Lentil Vegetable Soup   48
Turkey Barley Soup   49
Steamed Vegetables†   50
Toddler Vegetables†   51
Stir-Fried Vegetables†   51
Baked "French Fries"†   52
Hash Brown Potatoes   52
Salad†   53
Croutons†   54
Vinaigrette Dressing   54
Italian Dressing   54
Blue Cheese Dressing   55
Mayonnaise   55
Creamy Garlic Dressing†   56
Tartar Sauce†   56
Tomato Sauce   57
Pete's Pickles   57
Cranberry Relish†   58

CHAPTER 5   Dried Foods   59
Dried Mushrooms†   63
Dried Tomato Slices†   63
Dried Potato Pieces†   64
Dried Minced Onions†   64
Dried Carrots†   65
Dried Corn†   66
Dried Apples†   66
Dried Banana Slices†   67
Dried Peaches†   67
Dried Pears†   68
Dried Pineapple Rings and Pieces†   68
Fruit Leather†   70
Dried Herbs, Including Parsley and Oregano†   71

CHAPTER 6   Vegetarian Dishes   73
Vegetable Quiche   76
Lasagna   77
Stuffed Peppers†   77
Macaroni and Cheese   78
Pizza†   78
Quick Pizza   79
Potato Cheese Casserole   80
Bean Burritos   81
Vegetarian Stew   82
Rice   83
Beans   83
Sandwiches†   84

† indicates the recipe is either salt free or has no added salt.

CHAPTER 7   Meat, Poultry and Fish   85

    Chicken and Rice Bake   88
    Curried Chicken   88
    Barbequed Chicken   89
    Barbequed Spareribs   89
    Roast Turkey   90
    Bread Stuffing   90
    Crêpes with Turkey in Velouté Sauce   91
    Turkey Pot Pie   92
    Chicken Pot Pie   92
    Stir-Fried Chicken and Broccoli   93
    Sweet and Sour Pork   94
    Stir-Fried Pepper Steak†   95
    Egg Rolls   96
    Oriental Liver†   96
    Beef Stroganoff   97
    Savory Bean Casserole   97
    Risotto   98
    Potato Skillet Dinner   98
    Goulash   99
    Gyros   99
    Sloppy Joes   100
    Broiled Fish   100
    Crispy Baked Fish   101
    Fish Sandwich   101
    Tuna Fish Hotdish   102
    Toddler Meats†   102

CHAPTER 8   Snacks and Crackers   103

    Cheese Crackers   106
    Sesame Crackers   106
    Rye Crackers   107
    Graham Crackers   107
    Toddler Teething Crackers†   108
    Fresh Onion Dip†   108
    Blue Cheese Dip†   109
    Fruit Dip†   109
    Trail Mix†   109
    Carob Delight†   110
    Cheesy Popcorn†   111
    Sunflower Seed Snack†   111

CHAPTER 9   Desserts   113

    Apple Pie†   116
    Fresh Cherry Pie   116
    Pumpkin Pie   117
    Coconut Cream Pie   117
    Banana-Coconut Cream Pie   118
    Coconut Pudding   118
    Fresh Strawberry Cheesecake†   119
    Double Carob Cheesecake†   120
    Apple Nut Cake   121
    Banana Carob Chip Cake†   121
    Carob Cake†   122
    Carob Peanut Butter Frosting†   122
    Carrot Cake   123
    Cream Cheese Frosting†   124
    Christmas Fruitcake†   124

† indicates the recipe is either salt free or has no added salt.

Carob Dessert Crêpes 125
Carob Fudge Sauce† 125
Apple Crisp 126
Carob Brownies† 127
Vanilla Ice Cream 127
Carob Chip Ice Cream 127
Strawberry Ice Cream 128
Whipped Cream† 128
Super Fudge† 128
Caramels† 129
Halvah† 129
Carob Halvah† 130
Carob Treat† 130
Frozen Bananas† 130
Popsicles† 131
Yogurt Bars† 131
Yogurt Dream Bars† 132
Pina Colada Yogurt Bars† 132

CHAPTER 10 Cookies 133
Oatmeal Raisin Cookies 136
Peanut Butter Cookies 136
Carob Chip Cookies 137
Christmas Cookies 138
Natural Food Coloring† 138
Carob Pinwheels 139
Coconut Macaroons† 139
Gingerbread Cookies 140
Three-In-One Cookie 140
Fig Bars 141
Scotch Shortbread† 141
"Eagle" Bars† 142
Strawberry Apple Bars† 143
Peanut Butter Balls† 143

CHAPTER 11 Beverages 145
Herbal Tea† 148
Iced Tea† 148
Sun Tea† 148
Hot Russian Tea† 149
Mulled Cider† 149
Apple Banana Drink† 150
Citrus Cooler† 150
Melon Juice† 150
Tropical Delight† 150
Tomato Juice 151
Banapple Yogurt Milk Shake† 151
Strawberry Banana Milk Shake† 151
Orange Milk Shake† 152
Vanilla Milk Shake† 152
Strawberry Milk Shake† 153
Carob Milk Shake† 153
Hot Carob† 153
Instant Hot Carob† 154
Eggnog† 154

APPENDIX Natural Food Distributors 157
Recommended Reading 158

INDEX 159

† indicates the recipe is either salt free or has no added salt.

INTRODUCTION

As the general public becomes aware of how diet and health are inseparably related, more people make the change to natural foods. The reasons are obvious. A natural diet is high in fiber, low in fat and salt, free of chemical additives and contains no white sugar. For those concerned about their health, longevity and well-being (both physically and mentally), a change to natural foods is an obvious move. We are flooded with medical reports and personal testimonials attributing improved health, vigor and simply feeling better to various natural foods. Weight control is much easier when one eats filling whole foods.

This cookbook is designed to provide health-giving natural food recipes to those seeking an improved diet, but without sacrificing taste, flavor and one's favorite foods. Most of the recipes are already family favorites like Lasagna, Quiche, Barbequed Chicken, Chili, Pizza, Cinnamon Caramel Rolls and desserts such as Vanilla Ice Cream, Apple Pie, Fresh Strawberry Cheesecake, Peanut Butter Cookies and Carrot Cake.

None of the recipes include any refined flours or white sugar in any form. The use of salt is low or totally eliminated. The main dish recipes that include meat always call for lean cuts with all fat removed, and most recipes are low in the use of butter or oil.

The recipes chosen for this book were the ones "everybody" liked in natural food cooking classes I taught, and those preferred by friends and family. The bread recipes in this book have impressed many skeptics with the moistness and delicious taste of whole grain breads. These recipes make it easy to convert anyone to a more natural diet.

I became interested in natural foods in 1973, when I purchased a vegetarian cookbook. Prompted to read labels, I was amazed to see the long list of ingredients and assorted chemical substances present in many of the foods I ate. As I began researching what the chemicals were and the various problems associated with them, I also studied the advantages of eating whole foods as close to the natural state as possible. I decided to experiment and give up all products that contained any sugar, refined flour or artificial ingredients. At first it seemed the grocery store had few things I could eat, but I became determined to re-create my favorite foods using only whole grains, honey and other natural ingredients. Thus began my creative cooking efforts. Many of these recipes were old favorites I formerly created with sugar, white flour and other refined and processed foods. I substituted, adapted and added to the original recipes until the result was as good, or better tasting than the original. Other recipes were simply ideas, like Carob-Peanut Butter Granola; it just sounded good. I believe food should be enjoyed and not eaten simply because it's good for you. If it doesn't smell and taste delicious it's not worth it.

The recipes in this book will provide you with conclusive evidence that natural *is* better.

CHAPTER ONE

Making a Change for the Better

CHAPTER ONE

Making a Change for the Better

The increasing concern among Americans for our personal health includes a close scrutiny of the ways diet contributes to our health. Our search has brought us from fad and fashion through science labs into corporate boardrooms, as big business rushes to satisfy our changing requirements. This book is intended for anyone considering a more natural diet—one with less fat, cholesterol, salt, refined flours and sugar, a diet richer in fiber, whole foods and nutritional value.

The term "natural foods" has become synonomous with better eating nutritionally, but it is apparent that the term has various meanings, especially to the food industry. In this book, "natural" means unsynthetic, unadulterated and unrefined. This excludes white and brown sugars, white flour, margarine, etc. A "natural" food should not contain any synthetic ingredients and it should be as close to the whole, original food source as possible.

When purchasing foods, examine the label "natural" carefully. There appear to be no stringent guidelines followed by manufactureers, as many foods labeled "all natural" contain more additives, sugars and refined flours than the "regular" supermarket foods. The key is to check the ingredient list on each product you purchase and select those foods that are in accordance with your dietary requirements. Also consider that sugar has many names, such as dextrose, corn syrup, malt syrup, etc. "Wheat bread" may consist of unbleached white flour with caramel coloring and a small amount of whole wheat flour. If it doesn't say 100% whole wheat, it probably isn't.

When preparing the recipes in this book, a number of ingredients will need to be purchased. Since whole foods do not contain preservatives and many should be refrigerated, it's best not to purchase large amounts at first. All whole grain flours should be kept refrigerated or frozen until ready to use. Maple syrup, nuts, peanut butter, tamari, wheat germ, vegetable oils and dried fruits should be refrigerated also. Whole grains (unground), dried beans, bran, honey and molasses do not need to be refrigerated, but should be kept in tightly closed containers, safe from insects. Storing foods in labeled glass containers keeps foods easy to find and use.

The following categories list and describe staples necessary for cooking with natural foods.

GRAINS AND FLOURS

Whole Wheat Flour: whole wheat berries are ground to form the flour which includes not only the white starchy endosperm, but the bran and germ as well. Whole wheat bread flour is ground from hard wheat which is high in gluten and produces elastic dough. Whole wheat pastry flour is ground from soft wheat and is lighter, less glutenous and suitable for cakes and pastries.

Wheat Germ: the heart of the whole wheat berry, wheat germ contains most of the protein, iron, minerals, B and E vitamins found in wheat.

Bran: the outer layers of the wheat, bran is an excellent source of fiber, it's highly touted for aiding the digestive process.

Cornmeal: choose undegerminated or whole cornmeal that still contains the vitamin and protein-rich embryo or germ. Produces a coarser, crumbly baked product.

Rye Flour: baked goods with rye, mixed with whole wheat, will be tangy, moist and dense.

Carob Powder: a chocolate-like substitute, carob is a seed pod which is ground into a fine powder. It has almost no fat and is high in fiber and rich in vitamins and minerals. It's also sweet, unlike cocoa, and much less sweetener is needed in recipes, and carob contains no caffeine. Carob is available in hot drink mixes, baking chips, candy and baked goods as well as in powder form.

Rice Flour: ground from whole brown rice, rice flour gives baked goods a moister, sweeter taste and increases the nutritional value of foods.

Brown Rice: brown rice has the outer coating or "polish" that gives it a nuttier, heartier taste compared to white rice. The polish also provides essential fiber.

Barley: "unpearled" barley has more protein, potassium, calcium and iron than conventional "pearled" or refined barley.

Rolled Oats: purchase at a food co-op or natural foods store or buy the "Old Fashioned" variety at the supermarket.

SWEETENERS

Honey: composed of fructose and glucose (not sucrose), honey is a complex carbohydrate complete with vitamins, minerals and enzymes. There are a variety of different naturally flavored honeys to choose from, such as wildflower, clover, tupelo etc. Darker honeys are richer, more flavorful and contain more vitamins and minerals.

Molasses: unsulphered "Blackstrap" molasses is the most nutritious. Molasses has high iron content and is rich in vitamins and minerals.

Maple Syrup: use 100% pure maple syrup in all recipes requiring maple syrup, not pancake syrup which is 97% sugar and 3% maple flavoring.

Dried Fruit: unsulphered, unsweetened raisins, dried dates, figs, pineapple, bananas and apple slices are used to sweeten many desserts and baked goods.

PROTEIN SOURCES

Cheese: undyed (natural white or cream color) varieties such as mozarella, brick, monterey jack, swiss and parmesan. In larger stores it is possible to find undyed cheddar, colby and other cheeses as well.
Cultured Cottage Cheese: lowfat.
Skim or Low-fat Milk.
Unflavored Yogurt: made with cultured milk, not gelatin and additives.
Non-fat Dry Milk Powder.
Butter: pure sweet cream butter.
Eggs: from free-range poultry if possible.
Meat: nitrate free, unprocessed. Organically raised meat is preferable.
Peanut Butter: look for the kinds that contain "only peanuts", without sugar, fats or other unwanted ingredients. Select from salted or unsalted, chunky or smooth.
Nuts: raw almonds, cashews, walnuts, pecans, sunflower seeds, etc. Also dry roasted, unsalted peanuts.
Beans: dried pinto beans, kidney beans, Great Northern beans, lima beans.
Lentils: choose brown or orange.

FRUITS AND VEGETABLES

Always choose fresh when available and look for firm, unbruised select produce. Frozen is the next best alternative.

The best source for produce is your own garden, especially if you implement organic gardening methods. Organically grown produce is advantageous because you do not consume any pesticides, herbicides or fertilizers commonly found in commercially grown produce. For more information, refer to the list of organic gardening books listed in the appendix.

Fruit Juice: 100% pure fruit juice, unsweetened, without any coloring or flavoring. There is a wide variety including pear, peach, apple, grape, pineapple and strawberry.

COOKING OILS

Choose unrefined, pressed, vitamin rich oils. Compared to most commercial oils extracted with chemical solvents, unrefined oils are rich in taste, vitamins and minerals.

Safflower oil is a mild and general purpose cooking oil. Corn, peanut and almond oils are aromatic and tasty varieties to try also.

CONDIMENTS AND BAKING NEEDS

Sea Salt: contains naturally occurring minerals and does not include silica, dextrose or other additives found in table salt.

Tamari: a traditional form of soy sauce that contains only soybeans, wheat and salt without monosodium glutamate.

Active Dry Yeast: preservative free.

Baking Powder: aluminum-free.

COOKWARE AND APPLIANCES

Stainless Steel or Cast Iron Cookware: preferable for general cooking. Aluminum can leach out into the food especially if the food is acidic, like tomatoes.

Non-stick Cookware: time-saving way to cook eggs and everything else fat free.

Glass Bakeware: fine to use, but remember to decrease the temperature required in the recipes by 25°F.

Vegetable Steamer: an inexpensive way to get the most nutrition and flavor when cooking vegetables.

Yogurt Maker: an excellent investment to make yogurt for pennies a cup.

Ice Cream Maker: the best way to have additive-free ice cream.

Food Processor: great time-saver in the kitchen, especially the processors that knead bread.

Blender: useful for beverages and desserts as well as other food preparation if you don't have a food processor.

Pasta Maker: for uniform and inexpensive pasta.

Dehydrator: another good investment for drying bulk fruits and vegetables when they are in season and lowest in price. It also can be used for making yogurt and cheese.

Grain Mill: the most inexpensive method to obtain high quality flour with optimum freshness. Most grain mills can be adjusted to vary the texture from very fine to simply cracking the grains. The whole wheat berries can be purchased through co-ops, grain elevators and natural food stores.

Hot Air Popcorn Popper: excellent way to get a salt-free, low calorie snack without any oil. Even with a small amount of butter, this snack has fewer calories than the hot oil method of popping corn.

Whole Wheat Bread, Cinnamon Raisin Caramel Rolls and Corn Bread

CHAPTER TWO

Breads

CHAPTER TWO

Breads

A basic and integral part of our lives, bread's versatility is unmatched, and nothing else can compare to its aroma and flavor fresh from the oven.

Whether you choose to purchase flour, or grind your own flour for optimum freshness, remember the texture and fineness of the flour will make a difference on how your breads turn out. A very finely ground whole wheat flour will yield baked goods that are very light and moist. Walnut Acres in Pennsylvania is a natural food mail order outlet that sells a high quality of flour that is very finely ground. Walnut Acres' address as well as other natural food suppliers are listed in the appendix. Most commercially available whole wheat flour is much coarser, and produces a heavier, heartier tasting loaf. Try both to determine which you prefer.

All bread recipes can be made in a no-salt version without any noticeable change in appearance or texture, simply by omitting the salt.

To bake a successful loaf of bread, always follow these basics. First, read the entire recipe before beginning and then arrange all the ingredients called for on the counter so they're ready for use. Measure all the ingredients accurately and add them in the order listed. Since whole grain flours should be refrigerated, it's a good idea to warm them on your oven's lowest setting for a few minutes before mixing. This prevents cooling the dough and slowing down the yeast's action. Also when making yeast bread, be sure to have a warm enough place for the bread to rise, at least 80°F. but less than 100°F. Hotter temperatures can kill the yeast, preventing the bread from rising at all; cooler temperatures make the rising process much longer. For fastest rising, preheat your oven to the lowest setting, then turn the heat off, allow most of the heat to escape, and then place the dough inside. Using this method, the temperature is about 100°F. when you first place the dough in the oven, but the oven gradually cools down. Another good place to let bread rise is near a wood stove.

When the recipe calls for kneading the dough, knead vigorously for about 15 minutes or until the dough is very elastic and springs back when lightly tapped. After the second rising, the dough should double in size. To check for this, lightly press the dough. If it is done rising an indentation should remain.

Always preheat your oven before baking. Make sure the oven temperature is correct by using a thermometer and place baked goods in the center of the oven to properly circulate heat and prevent burning or over-browning on one side. To produce a nicely textured loaf, it is important not to over-bake, as this dries out the bread, or underbake, which leaves it raw in the center. Look for a nice golden brown top, and let the time listed in the recipe guide you as you gain expertise.

Baked goods store best sliced and frozen, unless you plan to eat them within several days. You may refrigerate bread for a week or more, but it seems to toughen it and it never tastes as fresh as frozen bread. Simply remove the bread from the freezer a slice at a time, allow for a few minutes thawing time or toast at once. Of course, in most homes fresh bread rarely lasts more than two days, and most of it disappears while still warm. Fresh, home-baked bread is always a treat.

WHOLE WHEAT BREAD

This is one of the fastest, tastiest double-rise whole wheat breads you can make. The rising time is only half as much as with conventional recipes, due to the fact that only half the flour is added to the yeast mixture for the first rising. The salt, oil and remaining flour are then added and kneaded as usual. You can have fresh yeasted bread in a little more than two hours!

⅓ cup honey

3 cups warm water (105°F.)

1½ tablespoons active dry yeast

8–9 cups whole wheat flour

1 cup nonfat dry milk powder (optional)

¼ cup safflower oil

1 tablespoon salt

In a very large bowl, mix the honey and water so the temperature equals 105°F. If it is cold in your kitchen, start with fairly hot water to warm the bowl and the honey. Remove the flour from the refrigerator and warm to at least room temperature. Stir the yeast and milk powder into the water and honey until dissolved. The milk powder adds moistness and protein to the bread, but may be omitted by those who have allergies to milk. Bread made without milk has a thicker, crisper crust. Now add 3¾ cups of flour, beat 100 strokes then cover with a damp cloth and allow to rise in a warm place. Let rise until doubled, about 30–35 minutes, then stir in the salt and oil. At this stage add any spices, fruit or nuts listed in the variations. Now slowly add the rest of the flour until you have a stiff, kneadable mass. Kneading is an important part of bread making, as the loaf will be heavy and will not rise very high unless you knead well. Kneading usually takes 10–20 minutes depending on the amount of gluten in the flour and the effectiveness of your kneading. Use either your knuckles or your palms, turning outside edges into the center continuously. Knead vigorously. Add flour to the mass as you knead to keep the dough from sticking to your hands, but keep it to a minimum to make sure the bread will be moist and light. You are done kneading when the dough is smooth and very elastic, springing back when lightly tapped.

Shape the dough into two equal loaves and place in two generously buttered loaf pans. Cover the pans with oiled wax paper and allow to rise in a warm place again for 40–45 minutes or until doubled. Lightly touch the dough and if an indentation remains, you are ready to bake. If you let it rise too long, it will begin to collapse. Should this happen, bake as usual, the flavor will be fine, but the appearance won't be pretty. Bake in a preheated oven at 350°F. for 30 to 35 minutes until nicely brown. Cool on wire racks. Makes 2 loaves.

VARIATIONS: • Use ⅓ cup molasses instead of honey.
  • Use ⅓ cup frozen orange juice concentrate instead of honey.
  • Add 1 teaspoon of your favorite spice.
  • Add ½ cup of chopped nuts or dried fruit or a combination of both.

CINNAMON RAISIN BREAD

Follow the basic Whole Wheat Bread recipe with the following changes. Increase honey to ⅔ cup. Add 2 beaten eggs when you are adding the salt and oil. Knead as usual, divide into two pieces and roll each out to about a ½ to ⅝ inch thickness in a rectangular shape. The length of one side should not exceed 9 inches in order to fit in the loaf pan. Brush the dough with 2 tablespoons melted butter per loaf, then drizzle with honey. Use up to ¼ cup of honey for each loaf. Sprinkle each with 1 tablespoon of cinnamon and then ½ cup of raisins. You may use more than ½ cup raisins per loaf if you like.

Now, very carefully roll the dough beginning with the 9 inch side. Roll the dough as tightly as you can, pinching the ends together as you go. When you get to the end, gently pinch the dough down on top of the loaf to seal. Fit in 2 buttered loaf pans, turning the ends under if slightly too long. Cover with oiled wax paper, let rise and bake as directed in the Whole Wheat Bread recipe. Terrific! Makes 2 loaves.

CINNAMON RAISIN CARAMEL ROLLS

These are so good it takes great self-control not to stuff yourself!

Follow the basic Cinnamon Raisin Bread recipe with the following changes. Divide the dough in half and roll each out into long rectangles about 10 inches wide and 15 inches long. Brush each with butter, drizzle with honey and sprinkle with cinnamon and raisins as in the bread recipe. Now carefully roll up the dough tightly to form a long narrow roll, beginning with the 15 inch side.

Prepare two 9 × 13 inch pans by buttering the sides and melting 3 tablespoons of butter in the bottom of each. Then drizzle 3 tablespoons of honey over the melted butter in each pan. Now cut the rolled-up dough in inch-thick slices and place in the pans. Cover with oiled wax paper and allow to rise in a warm place for 40–45 minutes or until doubled. Bake in a preheated oven at 350°F. for 30 minutes or until golden brown. Remove from the oven, loosen sides and turn entire pans upside down on a wire rack. Allow to cool for five minutes, then lift off pans. Serve hot or cold and be prepared for rave reviews. Makes 30–36 rolls.

WHOLE WHEAT ROLLS

Follow the basic Whole Wheat Bread recipe. When dividing the dough into two loaves, continue to divide each loaf into 12 or 16 pieces and shape into balls. If you choose 12 rolls, they will of course be larger than if you make 16. Butter two 9 inch square or springform pans. Press the top of each roll into a bowl of poppy seeds or sesame seeds, if desired, before placing in the pans. Cover the rolls with oiled wax paper and allow to rise, as in the Whole Wheat Bread recipe. Bake for 25 to 30 minutes in a preheated oven at 350°F., or until golden brown. Makes 24–32 rolls, depending on size.

ONION BREAD

Follow the basic Whole Wheat Bread recipe, but stir in a cup of freshly minced onion when you stir in the salt and oil. What an aroma! Great with cheese. Makes 2 loaves.

PUMPERNICKEL BREAD

Follow the basic Whole Wheat Bread recipe with the following changes. Use ¼ cup molasses and 3 tablespoons honey instead of all honey. After the first rising, add 3 cups of rye flour and 1 tablespoon of caraway seed along with the salt and oil. Add more whole wheat flour as needed (about 1¼ cups to 2¼ cups) to make a kneadable mass. Then knead as usual and follow the rising and baking directions in the Whole Wheat Bread recipe. Delicious with swiss cheese, lettuce and tomato! Makes 2 loaves.

ENGLISH MUFFINS

Delicious at breakfast or any time of day, these do not require oven baking, which makes them especially pleasing in the summer.

2 cups warm water	**5½–6 cups whole wheat flour**
2 tablespoons honey	**2 teaspoons salt**
1 cup nonfat dry milk	**¼ cup cornmeal**
1½ tablespoons dry active yeast	

Combine the warm water, milk and honey, then stir in the yeast until dissolved and well mixed. Add 2¾ cups of the flour and stir about 100 times, or until the lumps are gone and the dough is smooth. Cover the bowl with a damp cloth and place it in a warm spot to rise. Allow the dough to rise 30–35 minutes or until doubled. Now add the salt and stir well, then gradually add the rest of the flour until you have a kneadable mass. Continue to knead and add flour when necessary until the dough is elastic and springs back when lightly tapped. Roll out the dough on a lightly floured board to a ½ inch thickness. Cut into 3 inch circles using a round pastry cutter or an inverted glass, and place on a baking sheet that has been lightly sprinkled with cornmeal. Leave at least 2 inches between muffins. Cover with oiled wax paper and then a damp cloth and allow to rise in a warm place again for 40–50 minutes, or until doubled. Meanwhile heat a griddle to 275°F. Cook the muffins on the ungreased griddle for 10 minutes on each side, or until puffed and golden brown. Split with a fork to retain the distinctive texture when ready to eat. Makes 20 muffins.

CINNAMON RAISIN ENGLISH MUFFINS

Follow the same basic recipe for English Muffins, with the following changes. When stirring the salt into the dough after the first rising, add 1 tablespoon cinnamon and ⅔ cup raisins. Blend well then add the flour and follow the basic recipe for English Muffins. Makes 20 muffins.

WHOLE WHEAT EGG BAGELS

Delicious with cream cheese, tomato, lettuce and onion, or simply by themselves.

3 cups warm water
⅓ cup honey plus 2 tablespoons
4 eggs, beaten
1½ tablespoons dry active yeast

about 9 cups whole wheat flour
¼ cup oil
1 tablespoon salt
2 egg yolks, beaten

Combine the warm water, ⅓ cup honey and eggs, then stir in the yeast until dissolved and well mixed. Add 4 cups of the flour and beat 100 strokes, then cover with a damp cloth and allow to rise in a warm spot—80°F. to 90°F. is ideal. Let rise for about 30–35 minutes or until doubled. Now stir in the oil and salt, mixing well. Gradually add more flour, stirring until you have a kneadable mass. Knead for 10–20 minutes, adding flour when necessary to keep the dough from sticking to your hands. You are done kneading when the dough is very elastic and springs back when touched. Divide the dough into 36 equal pieces and roll each into a smooth ball. Now roll each ball into a strand about 6-7 inches long. Moisten the ends with water and form a circle. Place the dough circles on floured boards or trays and allow them to rise in a warm place for about 30 minutes, or until almost doubled in size. In a large kettle heat 4 quarts of water to boiling and stir in 2 tablespoons of honey. Place 4 bagels in the boiling water, and boil for 3 minutes, turning them over as they rise to the surface. Remove them with a slotted spoon and place on oiled or buttered baking sheets. Now place four more bagels in the boiling water, and continue until all have been boiled. Brush the tops of the bagels with the 2 beaten egg yolks, then bake in a preheated oven at 425°F. for 20–25 minutes. If you use two baking sheets on different shelves, alternate their positions after 10 minutes to make sure the top sheet of bagels does not become overly brown and the lower sheet of bagels does not burn on the bottom. They will turn a dark golden brown and the outer crust should be slightly crisp with the interior chewy. Makes 3 dozen bagels.

CINNAMON RAISIN WHOLE WHEAT EGG BAGELS

Follow the basic Whole Wheat Egg Bagel recipe, but when stirring in the salt and oil also add 2 tablespoons cinnamon and 1¼ cup raisins. Then continue as with the basic recipe. This is the most popular version. Makes 3 dozen bagels.

ONION WHOLE WHEAT EGG BAGELS

Follow the basic Whole Wheat Egg Bagel recipe, but when stirring in the salt and oil also add ½ cup dried minced onions, or 1 cup freshly minced onions. In addition, after brushing with egg yolk, sprinkle the bagels with dried minced onion pieces, sesame seeds or poppy seeds. Makes 3 dozen bagels.

PITA BREAD

A simple Middle Eastern flat bread which forms a pocket when cut in half. Pita Bread is perfect for filling with cheese, vegetables, nut spreads, fruit or anything you want.

2 cups warm water
1 teaspoon honey
1½ tablespoon dry active yeast

5–6 cups whole wheat flour
1 teaspoon salt

Mix the water and honey together in a large bowl. Add the yeast and stir until dissolved. Now add 2⅔ cups of the flour and stir vigorously until well blended, or at least 100 strokes. Stir in the salt, mixing well, then gradually stir in the rest of the flour until you have a kneadable mass. Knead for about 15 minutes, or until the dough is very elastic and springs back when lightly tapped. Add just enough flour to keep the dough from sticking to your hands. Divide the dough into ten equal balls, and roll each of them out to about a 6–7 inch circle. They should be about ¼ inch thick. Now place them on lightly floured wax paper and allow them to rise in a warm place, covered with oiled wax paper and a damp cloth. Let the pitas rise for about 40–50 minutes, or until a mark remains when they're lightly touched. When the pitas have risen, lightly flour the tops, place top side down on ungreased baking sheets, and bake in a preheated oven at 500°F. for 5 minutes on the lowest rack in the oven. The pitas are done when they are puffy, resembling clam shells. Watch the oven temperature carefully to ensure success. Allow the pitas to cool on a wire rack, lightly covered with a dry cloth. Then store in the refrigerator or freezer inside an airtight container. For a hot sandwich, toast half a pita in a toaster or oven for a few minutes, then fill with your favorite foods. The inside of the pita bread will remain soft, but the outside will be crisp. Makes 10 pitas, enough for 20 sandwiches.

BOSTON BROWN BREAD

This is a guaranteed winner! It's very moist, soft and sweet enough to be a dessert bread. Because the only sweeteners are molasses and raisins, it's very nutritional and high in vitamins, minerals and protein.

1 cup whole cornmeal
1 cup whole wheat flour
1½ teaspoon baking soda
¾ teaspoon salt

1 cup raisins
½ cup molasses
1 cup yogurt
⅓ cup milk

Mix dry ingredients together, adding raisins last. Separate the raisins by coating them with the flour mixture and rubbing them between your fingers. Mix the wet ingredients well and add these to the dry mixture. Pour the batter into a buttered 2 quart mixing bowl. The traditional method calls for placing the batter in a buttered coffee can, but using a bowl makes a much prettier and easier to remove loaf. Now you need a large, covered kettle, large enough for the mixing bowl to fit inside. Then put four chopsticks or butter knives on the bottom of the pan, resting them on top of each other to form a square. This will provide a base for the mixing bowl to keep it from direct contact with the pan. Now cover the bowl tightly with aluminum foil and a rubber band around the edge to hold it in place. Pour ½ inch of water in the kettle, heat it to boiling, place the bowl inside, cover and steam the bread for 2 hours. Add more water when necessary. After 2 hours, remove the bread from the kettle, take off the aluminum foil, remove from the bowl and place on a cooling rack. This bread is best while it's still warm. Makes 1 loaf.

PUMPKIN BREAD

A great way to use a surplus of pumpkin from the garden. Moist and spicy!

3⅓ cups whole wheat flour	¼ teaspoon nutmeg
⅓ cup wheat germ	⅔ teaspoon salt
2 teaspoon baking soda	2 cups cooked & pureed pumpkin
1 teaspoon baking powder	¾ cup honey
2 teaspoons cinnamon	¼ cup molasses
½ teaspoon allspice	2 eggs, beaten
¼ teaspoon ginger	⅔ cup raisins

Combine all the dry ingredients, except raisins, in a big bowl and mix well. Then add raisins, coating them with the flour mixture and separating them with your hands until evenly distributed. Mix the wet ingredients in a separate bowl. Preheat the oven to 350°F. and butter two loaf pans. Combine wet and dry mixtures stirring well and spoon into the loaf pans. Bake for 50 minutes or until a toothpick inserted in the center comes out clean. Makes 2 loaves.

VARIATIONS: • Substitute chopped dates for the raisins.
• Add 1 cup chopped nuts to the batter before baking.

CORN BREAD

Simple, easy and wonderful with soups, stews and cheese.

2 cups whole ground cornmeal	1 teaspoon baking soda
* 1 cup whole rice flour	2 eggs, beaten
1 teaspoon salt	2 cups yogurt

Rice flour combined with the cornmeal provides a natural sweetness, while the eggs and yogurt make it very moist. Combine the dry ingredients in a large bowl then stir in the eggs and yogurt. Pour into a buttered 9 inch square pan or cast iron skillet and bake in a preheated oven at 400°F. for 25 minutes or until golden brown. Serve with honey, butter or cream cheese. Serves 8.

VARIATIONS: • Add 1 cup of chopped fresh pineapple or drained, unsweetened, crushed pineapple.
• Add 1 cup steamed corn to the batter before baking.

* Note: Whole wheat flour may be substituted for rice flour if necessary.

GINGERBREAD

Super-moist, rich and an excellent source of iron.

2½ cups whole wheat flour
½ teaspoon salt
1 teaspoon baking powder
2 teaspoons cinnamon
2 teaspoons ground ginger

¼ teaspoon allspice
¾ cup molasses
⅓ cup safflower oil
1 cup yogurt
1 egg, beaten

Mix the wet and dry ingredients separately. Preheat the oven to 350°F. and butter a 9 inch square baking pan. Combine the wet and dry ingredients, pour into the pan and bake for 35 minutes or until a toothpick inserted in the center comes out clean. Cut into squares and serve with vanilla ice cream or yogurt. Makes 16 servings.

CARROT COCONUT BREAD

Very sweet and chewy.

3 eggs, beaten
⅓ cup safflower oil
⅔ cup honey
1 teaspoon vanilla
2 cups shredded carrots
1 cup unsweetened coconut
1 cup raisins

1 cup walnuts
½ teaspoon salt
1 teaspoon baking soda
1 teaspoon baking powder
2 teaspoons cinnamon
2 cups whole wheat flour

Mix eggs, oil, honey and vanilla together, then add carrots, coconut, raisins and walnuts. Stir well. Combine the rest of the ingredients and stir in the carrot mixture, until well blended. Spoon into a buttered loaf pan and bake in a preheated oven at 350°F. for one hour, or until a toothpick inserted in the center comes out clean. Remove from pan and cool. Keep refrigerated. Flavor improves after 24 hours. Makes one loaf.

BANANA BREAD

An old favorite, made better.

1½ cups whole wheat flour
¼ cup wheat germ
½ teaspoon salt
1 teaspoon baking soda
2 cups mashed ripe banana or about 4 bananas

½ cup honey
3 medium sized eggs, beaten
¼ cup safflower oil
1 teaspoon vanilla
¾ cup chopped walnuts

Mix dry and wet ingredients separately, setting the walnuts aside. Preheat the oven to 350°F. and butter a loaf pan. Combine the wet and dry ingredients, then fold in the walnuts. Pour into the loaf pan and bake for 1 hour, or until a toothpick inserted in the center of the loaf comes out clean. Cool 10 minutes in the pan and finish cooling on a wire rack. Makes 1 loaf.

VARIATION: • Substitute almonds for walnuts.

BANANA NUT MUFFINS

Follow the Banana Bread recipe with the following changes. Use only 3 bananas and 2 eggs. Mix as directed and place in 16 oiled muffin cups. Bake in a preheated oven at 350°F. for 25 minutes or until the muffins test done with a toothpick. Makes 16 muffins.

BRAN MUFFINS

A delicious high-fiber muffin for breakfast or a snack.

2 cups bran
1 cup whole wheat flour
1 teaspoon salt
1 teaspoon baking soda

¾ cup milk
½ cup yogurt
½ cup molasses
1 egg, beaten

Mix dry ingredients and wet ingredients separately. Preheat the oven to 375°F. and butter a muffin pan. Combine wet and dry ingredients, mixing well, and spoon into the muffin pan. Bake for 20 minutes. Makes 12 muffins.

BISCUITS

Good with stews, soups or by themselves.

2 cups whole wheat flour
1 tablespoon baking powder
½ teaspoon salt

¼ cup safflower oil
about ¾ cup milk
¼ cup sesame seeds

Mix the flour, baking powder and salt, then add the oil and stir again. Add just enough milk to make a soft dough that is not sticky, stirring lightly. Roll out to ¾ to 1 inch thick and cut with a biscuit cutter, inverted glass or cookie cutters. Children prefer the novelty of cookie cutter shaped biscuits. Sprinkle the biscuits with sesame seeds, place on a buttered baking sheet and bake in a preheated oven at 450°F. for 20 minutes or until golden brown. Makes about 16 biscuits.

CRÊPES

For a spectacular dinner or dessert there is nothing quite like crêpes. These paper-thin, moist pancakes store well in the refrigerator or freezer so you can prepare them in advance. They are not hard to make if you follow the directions, so try them and impress your friends!

4 large eggs
1¼ cups skim milk
½ teaspoon vanilla
2 teaspoons honey

1 cup sifted whole wheat flour
⅛ teaspoon salt
3 tablespoons melted butter

Beat the eggs, milk, vanilla and honey together until foamy. A blender works well. Now stir in the flour and salt and blend until well mixed. When smooth, add the cooled, melted butter and blend for a few seconds longer. Make sure you scrape the sides to ensure even blending. Now allow the mixture to rest, untouched, for 2–12 hours in the refrigerator. About ½ hour before you plan to make the crepes, remove the batter from the refrigerator and allow it to warm to room temperature. Preheat an 8 inch (bottom dimension) crêpe pan or skillet with sloped sides. Cast iron skillets also work well, if they have been properly seasoned. (To season a skillet, place a layer of oil and salt in the bottom and place over high heat. When the oil begins to smoke, remove all the oil and salt from the skillet and wipe clean with a cloth or paper towel.) Before cooking the crêpes, brush the pan lightly with oil and test by dropping a drop of water on the surface. When it sizzles the pan is ready. A medium-low setting keeps the pan at just the right temperature. Pour a scant ¼ cup of batter on the pan while holding the pan at a 45° angle. Immediately tip the pan from side to side to coat the bottom evenly. A smaller pan will require less batter. Return the pan to the heat and cook for about one minute until the top is set and the bottom is golden brown. Gently turn the crêpe over and cook for about 30 seconds longer, or until golden brown. The first side cooked will be prettier than the second, so when you fill the crêpes and roll them up, leave that side out. Stack the crêpes on a large plate as they are cooked, or serve them immediately. When cool, cover tightly with aluminum foil, keeping them flat, and refrigerate or freeze until ready to use. Be sure to remove them well ahead of when you plan to use them however, so they will be at room temperature before you roll them. Makes 14, 8 inch crêpes.

TORTILLAS

Make these for Bean Burritos, other sandwich fillings, or just to snack on.

2 cups whole wheat flour *or* 2 cups whole cornmeal
¾ teaspoon salt

2 tablespoons corn oil
⅔ cup hot water

Combine flour and salt then add the oil and water. Mix well and knead lightly. Divide into six balls and roll each out on a lightly floured board. Cook on a pancake griddle until the tortilla begins to bubble, then turn over and cook about 3 minutes more. This will make a soft shell tortilla. If you like crisp tortillas, cook them for 4 minutes or longer. Makes 6 large tortillas.

WHOLE WHEAT NOODLES†

Making your own noodles is incredibly easy and very economical. The texture is more bread-like and the flavor much better than commercially made noodles.

⅔ cup water   **whole wheat flour**
1 egg, beaten

Combine the egg and water. Begin adding flour slowly and work with your hands until the dough is no longer sticky, but not so dry that it will crack and tear apart. Roll out to about ⅛ inch and cut into strips for lasagna, small squares for casseroles or cut in a pasta machine. Allow to dry for several hours on a wire rack or towel. Cook in boiling water for 15–20 minutes. These can be frozen (before cooking) by placing them on a wire rack or cookie sheet in the freezer and then transferring them to a plastic bag when frozen. This prevents the formation of a large lump of frozen noodles. Cook the noodles from the freezer, allowing 2 minutes more cooking time.

VARIATIONS: • Use 2 eggs instead of 1 for rich egg noodles.
            • Omit the egg entirely.

† Salt Free.

BASIC PIE CRUST

1 cup whole wheat pastry flour   **¼ cup softened butter**
¼ teaspoon salt   **3–4 tablespoons ice water**

Mix salt and flour together and then cut butter in with a fork and knife or pastry cutter. Add the water slowly until it forms a ball. Do not overwork. Roll out on a lightly floured surface to about 12 inches in diameter. Carefully lift one side, fold it in half and lift into the pie plate, centering the fold in the center of the pan. Unfold, trim away the excess or flute the edges. If you need to bake the crust before filling, bake at 400°F. for 10 to 15 minutes. Prick the bottom with a fork before baking to prevent air bubbles. Makes 1 pie crust.

Orange Coconut Coffee Cake and Herbal Tea

TOMATO RYE PIE CRUST

This is very good with cheese and egg dishes, such as quiche.

½ cup rye flour
½ cup whole wheat flour
¼ teaspoon salt

¼ cup softened butter
¼ cup tomato juice, iced

Mix salt and flours together and then cut butter in with a fork and knife. Add the tomato juice slowly until the dough forms a ball. Roll out on a lightly floured surface to about 12 inches in diameter. Carefully lift one side, fold in half and lift into the pie plate or quiche pan, centering the fold. Unfold, trim away excess or flute edges. Bake at 400°F. for 10 to 15 minutes or fill first and bake according to the recipe being used. This also makes a delicious cracker if you roll it out, cut into squares, prick with a fork and bake as for the pie crust. Makes 1 pie crust.

COCONUT PIE CRUST†

Delicious, and smells wonderful when baking!

1 cup unsweetened coconut
⅓ cup whole wheat flour

⅓ cup wheat germ
3 tablespoons butter, softened

Combine the coconut, flour and wheat germ. Cut in the butter until well mixed. Press into a 9 inch pie plate and bake in a preheated oven at 350°F. for 12–15 minutes or until golden brown. This is great with a cream filling, but can be used for fruit or cheese pies too. Makes 1 pie crust.

† No Added Salt.

CHAPTER THREE

Breakfasts

CHAPTER THREE

Breakfasts

Grandma was right: you need a good breakfast to get going. Even the experts seem to agree that breakfast may well be the most important meal you eat all day. That's why it is especially important to start your day with nutritious whole grains and other high-protein foods. Whole grains have a "staying power" to get you through the morning, and allow you to function at peak efficiency without midmorning hunger pains. So, be kind to your body and begin the day with a natural foods breakfast.

This chapter will provide you with a variety of tasty breakfast ideas. There are more selections under the "Breads" chapter, such as English Muffins, Cinnamon Raisin Caramel Rolls, Bagels and many others. Don't forget that any food that is good for you at dinner or lunch is also good for you at breakfast. If you enjoy pizza, chicken, or some other high-protein food for breakfast, go ahead and eat it. There are no rules concerning what must be eaten at breakfast, so feel free to experiment. Children seem to enjoy sandwiches especially at breakfast, and if you select a high-protein filler such as peanut butter, egg, or cheese, you've given them an excellent start for the day. Serve the sandwich with a glass of milk and a piece of fruit or a glass of juice, to complete a balanced meal. Just make sure you use whole wheat bread, such as the varities in the "Breads" chapter. Whatever your family likes best.

Some of the breakfast recipes that follow are sweet enough to be enjoyed as a dessert or snack other times of the day, but are grouped here as they are "traditional" breakfast foods. The Baked Apples and Orange Coconut Coffee Cake make lovely desserts. Yogurt, omelets and other egg dishes are fine at any meal, and the granola recipes are a great snack all day. So enjoy these naturally good whole foods whenever YOU like!

OMELET

You won't believe how light this omelet is!

4 egg yolks, well beaten
½ teaspoon salt
dash pepper

4 egg whites
3 tablespoons water
1 tablespoon butter

Combine the beaten egg yolks with the salt and pepper, beat well then set aside. Beat the egg whites and water together until they form stiff peaks. Melt the butter in a 10 inch seasoned skillet or omelet pan over medium low heat, and coat the bottom and sides up to the rim. Now carefully fold the yolk mixture into the beaten egg whites and spread the mixture in the skillet. Cook for about 4 minutes, or until the underside of the omelet is golden brown. Now place the skillet and eggs into a preheated oven at 300°F. for about 3 minutes, or until the top is set and somewhat stiff. Remove from the oven, slice the omelet part way through in the middle and fold over. Gently slide the omelet out and serve at once. Serves 3–4.

CHEESE OMELET

Follow the basic omelet recipe but sprinkle 1 cup grated monterey jack, swiss, cheddar, mozarella or other cheese on the omelet just before folding over. Serves 4.

VARIATIONS: • Add 1 cup warm steamed vegetables when adding the cheese.
 • Add 1 cup cooked strips of chicken, turkey or fish when adding the cheese, or ½ cup meat and ½ cup vegetables.

FRUIT OMELET

A delightful breakfast!

Follow the basic omelet recipe but add ¾ cup drained, unsweetened crushed pineapple or unsweetened chunky applesauce. Or add 1 apple, peach or pear, very thinly sliced and lightly drizzled with a teaspoon of honey and a sprinkling of cinnamon or nutmeg. Strawberries, blueberries and raspberries may also be used as filling, but use ½ cup berries to 2 teaspoons honey. Serves 3–4.

SCRAMBLED EGGS

Creamy, light and delicious.

3 eggs, well beaten
⅓ cup cottage cheese
2 tablespoons chopped green pepper

¼ teaspoon salt
dash pepper
2 tablespoons butter

Combine eggs and cottage cheese and mix well. Then add the green pepper, salt and pepper. Melt the butter in a fry pan over low heat, then pour in the egg mixture. Cook until creamy, stirring constantly. Serve with whole wheat toast or fresh bread. Serves 2.

VARIATIONS: • Omit the green pepper.
                • Add 2 tablespoons sautéed onion.

FRENCH TOAST†

A favorite breakfast.

2 eggs, beaten
½ cup milk
½ teaspoon cinnamon

2 teaspoons oil
4 slices whole wheat bread

Combine eggs, milk and cinnamon. Preheat a skillet to medium low temperature and lightly coat skillet with 1 teaspoon oil. Soak 2 slices of bread in the egg mixture and cook until brown on both sides. Then use the remaining oil to re-coat the pan, soak the last 2 slices of bread and cook until brown. Serve with 100% maple syrup or spread with peanut butter for a treat children love. Serves 4.

† No Added Salt.

PANCAKES

A wonderful way to begin the day and so good for you!

1 cup whole wheat flour
½ cup wheat germ
½ cup bran
½ teaspoon salt
1 tablespoon baking powder

1¼ cups milk
2 eggs, beaten
2 tablespoons oil
2 tablespoons honey
2 teaspoons molasses

Mix dry ingredients together. Lightly oil and preheat a griddle or skillet to a moderate temperature. Combine liquid ingredients then add dry ingredients to mixture, stirring as little as possible. Small lumps will remain. Ladle onto the griddle and flip when the pancakes are full of bubbles and the edges lose their shiny, wet appearance. Wait about 3 minutes then check to see if the second side is brown by lifting an edge. If not, cook another minute or two until both sides are golden brown. Serve with natural 100% pure maple syrup and butter. Or try apple butter, peanut butter or fresh fruit. Makes about 12, 4 inch pancakes.

VARIATION: • Add ¾ cup fresh or thawed frozen blueberries just before you ladle the batter onto the griddle. Fold the blueberries in very gently or the batter will turn a grayish-purple!

ORANGE COCONUT COFFEE CAKE

Wonderful orange taste and aroma. Moist and tender, with a crisp topping that's great for breakfast, dessert or snacking.

1½ cups orange juice
1 cup oat flakes
½ cup plus 1 tablespoon honey
¼ cup butter
3 large eggs, beaten
1 tablespoon freshly grated orange peel

1 teaspoon vanilla
1¾ cups whole wheat flour
1 tablespoon baking powder
½ cup nonfat milk powder
¼ teaspoon salt
1 cup unsweetened dried coconut

Heat the orange juice to boiling in a small sauce pan. Stir in the oats and cook for one minute, then take off heat and allow to cool, stirring occasionally. Combine ½ cup honey, 3 tablespoons soft butter and eggs and beat until foamy. Sift together the flour, baking powder, milk powder and salt. Fold the cooled oatmeal, 1 teaspoon grated orange peel and vanilla into the egg mixture very gently, then slowly add the flour mixture, stirring until well blended. Turn into a 9 × 13 inch baking dish that has been lightly oiled and dusted with flour.

Combine the coconut, 1 tablespoon melted butter, 1 tablespoon honey and 2 teaspoons of orange peel and mix well with your fingers. Then, crumble the mixture over the cake batter evenly. Bake in a preheated oven at 375°F. for 25–30 minutes or until the cake topping is golden brown and the cake tests done with a toothpick.

Note: Freshly grated orange peel makes all the difference, so please do not substitute. Use undyed oranges if possible. Serves 15.

BLINTZES

A favorite for many years, these are wonderful at any meal, or as a dessert.

2 eggs, beaten	**¼ teaspoon salt**
2 tablespoons honey plus 1 teaspoon	**1 teaspoon baking powder**
2 teaspoons vanilla	**2 cups ricotta cheese**
¾ cup milk	**2 egg yolks**
½ cup unflavored yogurt	**¼ cup finely chopped almonds (optional)**
1 cup whole wheat flour	**2 tablespoons butter**

In a medium-sized bowl combine the 2 eggs, 2 tablespoons honey, 1 teaspoon vanilla, ¾ cup milk and yogurt. Beat until light. Then add the flour, salt and baking powder, stir gently until mixed. Small lumps will remain. Lightly oil a crêpe pan or small skillet. Heat the pan to medium and pour about ¼ cup (scant) of batter into the pan, turning and tipping the pan to spread the batter over the entire bottom of the pan. Cook until the top of the pancake is dry, then turn and cook for about 30 seconds until brown on the other side. Place the pancakes on a damp towel as you make the others.

   Combine the cheese, egg yolks, teaspoon of honey and 1 teaspoon vanilla. Also add the chopped almonds, if desired. Put a heaping tablespoon of the egg mixture in the center of each blintz cake and fold, enclosing the filling like an envelope. Lightly oil a large skillet and melt the butter. Brown the blintzes on each side and serve warm with applesauce and cinnamon or fresh fruit and unflavored yogurt. Makes 12 blintzes, 6 servings.

INSTANT BLINTZ†

These are great when you are in a hurry but still want a special breakfast.

2 whole wheat pita breads or 4 slices whole wheat bread	**¾ cup ricotta or cottage cheese**
2 eggs	**2 teaspoons honey**
4 tablespoons milk	**½ teaspoon vanilla**
1 tablespoon butter	**cinnamon**

Trim the outer perimeter of the pita bread away, about ¼ inch or so, and separate the two layers. If you are using whole wheat bread, remove the outer crust and roll flat with a rolling pin. Beat the eggs and milk together and melt the butter in a large skillet. Combine the cheese, honey and vanilla. Dip each slice of bread in the egg mixture to thoroughly coat both sides. Spoon about 3 tablespoons of the cheese mixture in the center of each slice of bread, fold over and secure with a toothpick through one side. Cook over medium-low heat for about 3 minutes or until golden brown. Now remove the toothpicks, and turn over, cooking the second side about 3 minutes also. Serve hot with applesauce, sliced fresh bananas or crushed pineapple and lightly sprinkle with cinnamon if desired. Serves 4.

VARIATION: • Add 1 tablespoon chopped nuts or 1 tablespoon dried fruit pieces to the cheese mixture.

† No Added Salt.

CINNAMON RAISIN OATMEAL

A delicious way to get your kids to eat hot cereal.

1⅓ cups boiling water	**¼ teaspoon salt**
⅔ cup flaked oats	**⅓ cup raisins**
½ teaspoon cinnamon	**honey and milk**

Stir the oats, salt, cinnamon and raisins into the boiling water. Turn heat down to low and cook for about 5 minutes, stirring frequently. When thick, spoon into two bowls, drizzle with honey and pour milk over each. You can add more raisins as a topping; children especially like the raisins arranged in a face pattern. Serves 2.

VARIATIONS:
- Add 1–2 tablespoons wheat germ to the boiling water.
- Substitute ¼ cup chopped dates for the raisins.
- Add 2 tablespoons chopped nuts.

FRUIT AND NUT GRANOLA†

2 cups rolled oat flakes	**½ cup chopped almonds**
2 cups wheat flakes	**½ cup honey**
1½ cups wheat germ	**⅓ cup oil**
½ cup bran	**1 teaspoon vanilla**
¼ cup sesame seeds	**½ cup raisins**
½ cup unsweetened dried coconut	**½ cup chopped dates**
¼ cup raw sunflower seeds	**½ cup dried pineapple pieces**
½ cup chopped cashews	**½ cup dried apple pieces**

Mix together all ingredients in first column. Then stir in honey, oil and vanilla. Pour into a 9 × 13 inch baking dish and bake in a preheated oven at 325°F. for about 25 minutes. Stir every 7 minutes. Granola is done when it's golden brown all over. Remove from the oven and add the dried fruit while granola is still warm. Turn the mixture out on a clean towel, allow to cool and store in a tightly closed container. Makes about 10 cups granola.

† Salt Free.

MAPLE GRANOLA†

Extra crisp, with a sweet maple and almond flavor.

¼ cup oil
¼ cup honey
⅓ cup 100% maple syrup
1 teaspoon vanilla
2 cups rolled oats

2 cups flaked rye (or additional rolled oats may be substituted)
½ cup wheat germ
¾ cup chopped almonds
½ cup raisins

Mix together the oil, honey, maple syrup and vanilla. Then stir in the oats, rye, wheat germ and almonds. Stir well and place in a 9 × 13 inch baking dish. Bake in a preheated oven at 325°F. turning every 7–10 minutes until golden brown. It usually takes about 30 minutes. Then turn the granola out on a clean, dry towel and allow to cool. Add the raisins, stir well, and store in a tightly closed container. Makes about 5½ cups granola.

† Salt Free.

PEANUT BUTTER GRANOLA†

Wonderful as a snack as well as for breakfast.

½ cup honey
½ cup peanut butter
3 cups rolled oats
1 cup wheat germ

½ cup unsweetened dried coconut
¼ cup sesame seeds
1 tablespoon cinnamon
1 cup raisins *or* chopped dates

Combine the honey and peanut butter and warm slightly. Stir in the rest of the ingredients, except the raisins or dates, and place in a 9 × 13 inch baking pan. Bake in a preheated oven at 350°F., turning every 7–10 minutes until golden brown. It usually takes about 30 minutes. Now turn the granola out on a clean, dry towel and allow to cool. Add the dried fruit, stir well and store in a tightly closed container. Makes about 6 cups of granola.

VARIATIONS: • Add ¾ cup peanuts or almonds before baking.
  • Add 1 cup dried pineapple chunks after baking.

† No Added Salt.

CAROB-PEANUT BUTTER GRANOLA†

Tastes like a cookie or candy, but so much better for you!

Follow the Peanut Butter Granola Recipe with the following changes. Add ½ cup carob powder to the dry mixture. Omit the cinnamon and dried fruit.

† No Added Salt.

STRAWBERRY COCONUT GRANOLA†

The tangy strawberry flavor and aroma make this chewy granola a hit.

¾ cup strawberry preserves made with honey
¼ cup honey
2 tablespoons melted butter
2 tablespoons safflower oil
1 teaspoon vanilla
2½ cups rolled oat flakes

1 cup rye flakes *or* substitute another cup of
rolled oats
1¼ cup unsweetened dried coconut
1 teaspoon cinnamon
½ cup raisins

Combine the preserves, honey, butter, oil and vanilla in a large bowl, then stir in the remaining ingredients except the raisins. Mix well then pour in a 9 × 13 inch baking dish and bake in a preheated oven at 325°F. Bake the granola for about 30 minutes, or until golden brown, stirring every 7 minutes. Remove from the oven then mix in the raisins. Pour the granola out on a clean cloth and allow to cool, then store in a tightly closed container. Makes 5–6 cups granola.

VARIATION: • Add ½ cup dehydrated strawberries after baking!

† No Added Salt.

BROILED GRAPEFRUIT†

Wonderful on a cold winter morning.

1 grapefruit
honey

cinnamon

Cut the grapefruit in half crosswise, loosen sections from the membrane and remove the center core. Lightly drizzle honey over each half and sprinkle with cinnamon. Place in a baking dish and broil in a preheated oven 4 inches away from the heat for 7–10 minutes or until the tops become brown and bubbly. Serve hot with a lightly toasted and buttered English Muffin or Whole Wheat Bread. Serves 2.

† Salt Free.

BAKED APPLES†

An easy, nutritious breakfast or dessert.

4 large tart apples
¼ cup chopped almonds or walnuts
2 tablespoons raisins
2 tablespoons chopped dried dates

1 teaspoon cinnamon
2 tablespoons honey
2 teaspoons lemon juice
apple juice

Wash and core apples, but do not peel. Combine the nuts, dried fruit, cinnamon, honey and lemon juice and stir until well blended. Fill the apple hollows with the nut mixture and place in a shallow baking dish. Pour apple juice in the bottom of the dish up to a depth of ½ inch and bake in a preheated oven at 375°F. for about 45 minutes. Baste the apples with the juice two or three times while baking. Serve warm with vanilla ice cream or whipped cream when serving as a dessert or with unflavored yogurt for a breakfast sensation. Can also be served cold. Serves 4.

† Salt Free.

WINTER FRUIT SALAD†

A light, cheerful breakfast or dessert.

1 apple	**1 cup pineapple chunks**
1 orange	**1 pear**
½ grapefruit	**2 tablespoons orange juice**
1 banana	**¼ cup unsweetened dried coconut**

Wash all fruit, then peel the orange, grapefruit and banana. Cut all pieces into ½–1 inch thick pieces and toss with the orange juice and coconut. Serve with unflavored or honey-sweetened yogurt if desired. If you do not intend to serve at once, delay cutting the banana until just before you do serve to prevent softening and discoloring. Keep refrigerated. Serves 4.

† Salt Free.

SUMMER FRUIT SALAD†

Endless combinations are possible, but this is a favorite.

½ cantalope, skin removed	**1 orange, sectioned**
1 cup fresh strawberries	**½ cup pineapple chunks**
1 cup cubed watermelon	**1 peach, pitted**
⅔ cup sweet cherries, pitted	**⅔ cup seedless grapes**
1 plum, pitted	**3 tablespoons orange juice**

Wash all the fruit, and cut into ½–1 inch thick cubes except for the grapes which should be left whole and the cherries which should be cut in half. Toss with the orange juice until well mixed. Keep refrigerated. Serves 6.

† Salt Free.

SUNNY FRUIT COMPOTE†

Sweet and delicious for breakfast or a dessert.

1 cup dried apricot halves
1 cup dried prunes

1 cup unsweetened pineapple juice

Mix all the ingredients together, stirring well. Refrigerate for about 10–12 hours or until the fruit plumps up a bit. Now heat the mixture in a small saucepan until it boils, then simmer a few minutes. Serve hot or cold. Delicious with unflavored yogurt, sprinkled with chopped nuts or both. Serves 4–6.

† Salt Free.

SPICY FRUIT COMPOTE†

A winter favorite.

1 cup dried apple slices
½ cup raisins
½ cup dried pitted dates

1 cup apple juice, unsweetened
¼ teaspoon cinnamon
dash nutmeg

Mix all ingredients together, stirring well and refrigerate for about 10–12 hours or until the fruit plumps up a bit. Now heat the mixture to boiling in a small sauce pan and simmer for 5 minutes. Serve hot with chopped nuts and unflavored yogurt if desired. Serves 4–6.

† Salt Free.

Turkey Vegetable Soup and Salad

YOGURT†

Home-made yogurt is very simple and inexpensive to make. A yogurt maker is not essential, but is very helpful in maintaining the proper temperature. A dehydrator can also be used for making yogurt.

7 cups warm (110°F.) water
4 cups instant nonfat dry milk powder

¼ cup unflavored cultured yogurt

Mix the water and milk powder together until dissolved, then stir in the yogurt and mix well. Pour into pre-warmed yogurt maker containers or into four individual glass pint containers and cover. The yogurt maker or dehydrator will keep the mixture just the right temperature. However, if you don't have either appliance, simply place the yogurt filled containers in a warm place and cover them tightly with lots of towels or other insulating material, to maintain the 110°F. temperature. With a yogurt maker or dehydrator, the yogurt will be done in as little as 3–6 hours, possibly longer. With the towel method it may take over-night. The yogurt is done when it has set and is thick and firm. Refrigerate the yogurt when set, it will keep up to two weeks. Save ¼ cup of your yogurt to make the next batch so you won't have to buy more. Serve with fresh fruit or granola. Makes 2 quarts.

† Salt Free.

KIBBUTZ BREAKFAST†

In Israel a wide variety of foods are served banquet style and everyone can select their own breakfast. Simply set out plates and some, or all, of the following foods.

hard boiled eggs
sliced cheeses
yogurt
peanut butter and other nut butters
fish
breads and muffins
crackers
cottage cheese
milk
honey
fresh fruit in season

carrot sticks
cucumbers
olives
tomatoes
green pepper slices
onions
cabbage
radishes
salad dressings
tea
dried fruit

This general idea works well for most everyone. You don't have to worry about making something different for finicky family members, and after breakfast is over simply put the foods back in the refrigerator and they're ready for the next meal. While vegetables and fish might not be what you are accustomed to at breakfast, they are common fare in many regions throughout the world and so high in nutritional value you might want to consider adding them to your breakfast repertoire. Experiment!

† No Added Salt.

TODDLER BREAKFASTS†

Once you and your doctor have decided to let your child start solids, here are some nutritious ways to feed baby whole natural foods.

Hot Cereal: Buy coarsly ground whole wheat, oats, corn or rice meal. Cook 2 tablespoons of meal in ½ cup boiling water, milk or unsweetened fruit juice. Turn heat to low and cook, stirring frequently for 10 to 15 minutes or until the desired consistency is reached. Serve with a small amount of milk or fruit juice. Do not add sugar or salt.

Scrambled Eggs: Cook a beaten egg without adding salt or pepper over low heat until firm. Allow baby to eat as finger food.

French Toast: Prepare as in the adult recipe, but without salt or cinnamon. When done, cut off crust and slice in half. Spread one half with unsalted, natural peanut butter (peanuts only), and cover with second half of toast. Cut into strips about 1 inch wide. These "mini breakfast sandwiches" can be eaten as finger food.

† Salt Free.

CHAPTER FOUR

Soups, Vegetables and Condiments

CHAPTER FOUR

Soups, Vegetables and Condiments

An important part of most every meal, vegetables provide important vitamins, minerals and roughage as well as adding beautiful color and appeal.

Start with fresh vegetables whenever possible, and use them soon after buying. To preserve nutrients, taste, color and flavor, vegetables should be served raw, steamed or lightly stir-fried. Having your own garden is the best way to assure your vegetables are at the peak of freshness and grown without chemicals, sprays or fertilizers. You can pick dinner vegetables minutes before cooking for results that simply can't be beaten.

When winter arrives and your garden is no longer producing, fresh produce can still be purchased at supermarkets or farmer's markets. Frozen vegetables provide an excellent alternative when fresh is unavailable. Excess garden produce can be frozen to be enjoyed later.

Another alternative to fresh is dried vegetables which are especially useful in soups and casseroles. The following chapter will explain how to dry foods and cook with them. Dried foods have the advantage of letting you purchase foods when they are in season and lowest in price, and allowing you to preserve and store them for later use. This can be a big savings to families on a tight budget. You can also dehydrate excess garden produce, thus eliminating waste. Another advantage is that it can be simpler and faster to make soup. No need to wash, peel or chop—dried foods are ready to go. And of course hikers and campers have long appreciated the lightness and ease of traveling with dried vegetables and other foods.

Soups can be served as an addition to a main course or they can be the focus of the meal. The soups in this chapter are very thick, hearty and satisfying. Some of them look more like stew and are just as filling. There is nothing better on a cold winter's day than one of these soups and homemade crackers or bread just out of the oven. Always hits the spot.

TURKEY VEGETABLE SOUP

A favorite use for leftover turkey.

* **3 cups chopped or unsalted stewed tomatoes**
3 cups water
2 carrots, chopped
3 stalks celery, chopped
1 large potato, chopped
1 small onion, chopped
2 tablespoons dried parsley, crushed
* **2 teaspoons salt (decrease to 1 teaspoon if salted stewed tomatoes are used)**

½ teaspoon oregano flakes, crushed
1 teaspoon chili powder
¼ teaspoon garlic powder
1 cup frozen or fresh corn
½ cup frozen or fresh green beans
½ cup frozen or fresh lima beans
2 cups cooked turkey, cubed

Place all the ingredients except the corn, green beans, lima beans, and turkey in a large pot and bring to a boil. Turn down to simmer, cover and cook for 1 hour. Then add the corn, beans and turkey and bring to a boil again. Cover and simmer once more for 30–40 minutes, or until all the vegetables are tender. Serve with crackers or hot Corn Bread, refer to the index for the recipes. Serves 6.

Note: If you choose to substitute dried vegetables for any of the fresh vegetables called for in the recipe, substitute the following amounts. Add all dried vegetables at the beginning to ensure enough cooking time.

3 cups tomatoes	1½ cups dried tomato pieces plus 1½ cups water
2 large carrots	½ cup dried chopped carrots plus ½ cup water
3 stalks celery	¾ cup dried chopped celery plus ¾ cup water
1 large potato	½ cup dried chopped potato plus ½ cup water
1 small onion	2 tablespoons dried minced onion plus 2 tablespoons water
1 cup corn..........................	½ cup dried corn plus ½ cup water
½ cup green beans..................	¼ cup dried green beans plus ¼ cup water
½ cup lima beans	¼ cup dried lima beans plus ¼ cup water

CHILI

A terrific winter-day warmer-upper!

1 cup dried pinto beans
1 cup dried kidney beans
1 cup uncooked rice, rinsed
* 1 quart freshly chopped or stewed tomatoes,
unsalted
1 large onion, chopped
3 stalks celery, chopped

2 tablespoons dried parsley, crushed
2 tablespoons chili powder
* 2 teaspoons salt (decrease to 1 teaspoon if
salted stewed tomatoes are used)
1 teaspoon garlic powder
1½ teaspoon oregano flakes, crushed

Wash and pick through the beans and bring them to boil in 6 cups of water. Simmer for about 3 hours or until tender. Then add the remaining ingredients, 2 additional cups of water, and bring to a boil again. Simmer for 1 hour and serve with hot Corn Bread or Sesame Crackers, refer to the index for both recipes. Serves 6.

Note: If you choose to substitute dried vegetables for any of the fresh vegetables called for in the recipe, substitute the following amounts. Allow for 1 additional hour of cooking time.

1 quart tomatoes . . . . 2 cups dried tomato pieces plus 2 cups water
3 stalks celery . . . . ¾ cups dried chopped celery plus ¾ cup water
1 large onion . . . . ¼ cup dried minced onion plus ¼ cup water

CHICKEN NOODLE SOUP

Cures all "ills", especially hunger!

8 cups water
chicken parts, (5 wings, 3 backs or a similiar combination)
1 large onion, chopped
2 stalks celery, chopped
2 large carrots, chopped

2 tablespoons dried parsley, crushed
¼ teaspoon ground pepper
2 teaspoons salt
1 cup whole wheat ABC noodles or other whole wheat noodles

Place the chicken, onion and water in a large pot and bring to a boil. Cover and simmer 2 hours, then remove the chicken pieces. After allowing the chicken to cool to the touch, remove all the fat, skin and bone, and return the meat pieces to the pot. Then add the celery, carrots and spices and heat to boiling. Turn down and simmer for 1 hour, then stir in the noodles and allow to cook 1 more hour, or until the noodles are tender. Serves 6.

Note: If you choose to substitute dried vegetables for any of the fresh vegetables called for in the recipe, substitute the following amounts. Add all dried vegetables at the beginning to ensure enough cooking time.

1 large onion . . . . ¼ cup dried minced onion plus ¼ cup water
2 stalks celery . . . . ½ cup dried chopped celery plus ½ cup water
2 large carrots . . . . ½ cup dried chopped carrots plus ½ cup water

BEAN SOUP

Hearty, thick and tasty! Try it with Corn Bread (see index).

2 cups dried pinto beans	**2 stalks celery, chopped**
6 cups water, plus 2 cups later	**2 large carrots, chopped**
2 tomatoes, chopped	**½ teaspoon garlic powder**
½ cup uncooked brown rice	**1 teaspoon parsley**
2 tablespoons dried minced onion	**2 teaspoons salt**
¼ teaspoon oregano, crushed	**dash pepper**

Wash and sort through the beans to remove any foreign objects. Allow the beans to soak overnight in 6 cups of water, or bring the beans to a boil in the water. Now pour out all the water, no matter which method you chose. This tends to reduce the gassy effect beans have on many people. Add 6 cups of clean, hot water to the beans and bring to a boil. Cover and simmer, stirring occasionally, until tender. That will be about 2 hours if the beans were soaked overnight, or 4 hours if not soaked. Now remove 2 cups of cooked beans and put them in a blender with 2 cups of water and the tomatoes, and blend until smooth. Pour the mixture into a large kettle and add the rest of the ingredients. Bring the soup to a boil, then simmer, covered for 45–60 minutes, stirring occasionally. Serves 6–8.

VARIATIONS: • Add 1 cup of chopped cabbage when the other vegetables are added.
- Add 2 chopped potatoes instead of rice and subtract 1 cup water when blending the 2 cups of beans.
- Add corn, fordhook lima beans, green beans or any other vegetable.

Note: If you choose to substitute dried vegetables for any of the fresh called for in the recipe, substitute the following amounts. Allow for 1 additional hour of cooking time.

2 stalks celery	½ cup dried chopped celery plus ½ cup water
2 large carrots	½ cup dried chopped carrots plus ½ cup water
2 tomatoes	½ cup dried tomato pieces plus ½ cup water

LENTIL VEGETABLE SOUP

A delicious meal with rye crackers and cheese.

1 cup dried lentils
1 medium onion, chopped
2 stalks celery, chopped
3 large carrots, chopped
* 2 cups chopped or stewed tomatoes
   (unsalted)
½ cup fresh or frozen sweet corn

4 teaspoons dried parsley, crushed
* 1½ teaspoon salt (decrease to ½ teaspoon
   if salted stewed tomatoes are used.)
½ teaspoon garlic powder
½ teaspoon oregano flakes, crushed
2 tablespoons tamari

Wash and pick over lentils. Bring the lentils to a boil in 4 cups of water. Stir in the vegetables and add the spices. Bring to a second boil, then cover and simmer 2 hours. Stir occasionally. Serves 6.

VARIATIONS: • Add ½ cup uncooked, washed rice and 1 cup more water.
              • Add lima beans (fresh or frozen), green beans, or any vegetable you like.

Note: If you choose to substitute dried vegetables for any of the fresh vegetables called for in the recipe, substitute the following amounts.

1 medium onion	3 tablespoons dried minced onion plus 3 tablespoons water
2 stalks celery	½ cup dried chopped celery plus ½ cup water
3 large carrots	⅔ cup dried chopped carrots plus ⅔ cup water
2 cups tomatoes	1 cup dried tomato pieces plus 1 cup water
½ cup corn	¼ cup dried corn plus ¼ cup water

TURKEY BARLEY SOUP

Similiar to Scotch Broth in flavor, but uses turkey instead of lamb.

4½ cups water
*** 3 cups chopped or stewed tomatoes,
    unsalted**
¾ cup uncooked barley
2 cups diced cooked turkey
2 tablespoons dried minced onion

2 large carrots, chopped
2 stalks celery, chopped
1 tablespoon dried parsley, crushed
¼ teaspoon rosemary, crushed
*** 2 teaspoons salt (decrease to 1 teaspoon if
    salted stewed tomatoes are used)**

Heat the water and tomatoes to boiling, stirring in the turkey, barley, vegetables and seasonings. Allow to boil for a few minutes, then turn down to simmer and cook covered for 1½ hours or until the vegetables are tender. Serve hot with sesame or cheese crackers. Serves 6.

Note: If you substitute dried vegetables for any of the fresh vegetables called for in the recipe, substitute the following amounts.

3 cups tomatoes . . . . 1½ cups dried tomato pieces plus 1½ cups water
2 large carrots . . . . ½ cup dried chopped carrot plus ½ cup water
2 stalks celery . . . . ½ cup dried chopped celery plus ½ cup water

STEAMED VEGETABLES†

This is a preferable way to serve cooked vegetables, to retain the most flavor and preserve nutrients. Vegetables should be just tender, never soggy or limp. Here is a timetable for steaming various vegetables. Put about ¾ of an inch of water in the bottom of your pot, then the steamer, then the freshly washed and sliced vegetables, or frozen vegetables. If you use frozen vegetables, be sure to stir frequently at first to break up the vegetables and make sure they are evenly heated. You can save the water remaining after steaming is done, and add it to soups or stews as vegetable stock.

Artichokes	15–18 minutes
Asparagus	8–12 minutes
Beans (green or wax)	7–10 minutes
Beets, sliced	8–10 minutes
Broccoli pieces	7–10 minutes
Brussels Sprouts	10–14 minutes
Cabbage, sliced	5– 8 minutes
Carrots, sliced	8–10 minutes
Cauliflower pieces	7–10 minutes
Celery, sliced	7–10 minutes
Corn, cut	2– 4 minutes
Corn on the cob	6– 8 minutes
Green Pepper, sliced	5– 8 minutes
Kale	4– 6 minutes
Mushrooms, whole	12–14 minutes
Peas, shelled	5– 8 minutes
Potatoes, sliced	8–12 minutes
Spinach	3– 6 minutes
Squash, cubed	6–10 minutes
Tomatoes, sliced	3– 5 minutes
Turnips, sliced	8–12 minutes
Zucchini, cubed	7–10 minutes

When the vegetables are done sprinkle with grated parmesan cheese, salt lightly, or dot with butter if desired. You can sprinkle the vegetables with garlic, onion or other spices before cooking, or you can add herbs and spices to the water before steaming to flavor the vegetables. You'll be amazed at the wonderful flavor steamed vegetables have, especially if you are presently using canned products. Steamed vegetables can frequently be enjoyed with no seasoning whatsoever.

† Salt Free.

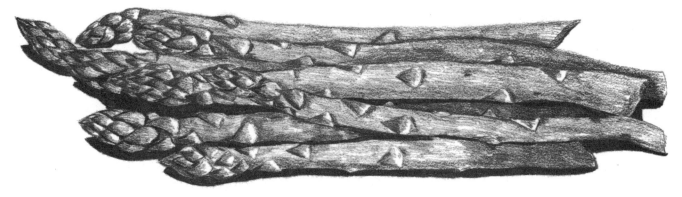

TODDLER VEGETABLES†

Steam vegetables until soft and very tender, about twice as long as the time required in the Steamed Vegetables listing. Grind the cooked vegetables in a blender, press through a sieve or use a baby food grinder. Do not salt, butter or season. When introducing vegetables to toddlers, begin with only one variety of vegetable at a time, and cook very small portions. Leftover vegetables may be stored for a few days in small containers in the refrigerator and rewarmed when needed. Another alternative is to freeze the pureed vegetables in ice cube trays and then transfer the frozen cubes to plastic bags in the freezer. You can then remove one or two "vegetable cubes" to be warmed at serving time.

Older toddlers may enjoy steamed vegetables that are well cooked without processing, such as tiny carrot strips, green beans and potato strips. Watch closely to prevent choking however and give only at your doctor's recommendation. Again, no salt, butter or seasoning.

Do not include tomatoes, which many are allergic to, or vegetables from the cabbage family such as broccoli and cauliflower, until the child is older and better able to tolerate them.

† Salt Free.

STIR-FRIED VEGETABLES†

Elegant, crisp vegetables to serve over brown rice or as part of a Chinese dinner.

1 medium onion	**2 tablespoons peanut or safflower oil**
1 carrot	**2 tablespoons tamari**
⅔ cup cabbage	**½ teaspoon honey**
1 stalk celery	**3 tablespoons chicken or vegetable stock**
1 pound bunch of fresh broccoli	**1 teaspoon cornstarch**
¼ pound fresh mushrooms	**1 cup fresh mung bean sprouts**
¼ pound fresh spinach leaves	

Wash all the vegetables. Chop the onion, carrot, cabbage and celery into ¼ inch pieces. Cut the broccoli flowers into bite sized pieces and chop the stems into ½ inch thick diagonal slices. Cut the mushrooms vertically about ½ inch thick. Cut the spinach leaves to about 2 inches square, so they can be eaten easily. Place the oil in a wok or large skillet and heat to medium-high, but not so hot that it smokes. Sauté the onions until golden then stir in the celery, carrot and broccoli and stir-fry for one minute. Add the tamari, honey, 2 tablespoons stock, mushrooms and cabbage, stir-fry for another minute, then cover and cook over moderate heat for 2 minutes. In a small cup, mix the cornstarch in the remaining stock. Stir the spinach and bean sprouts into the broccoli mixture. When well-mixed stir in the cornstarch mixture and stir until the vegetables are coated with a light glaze. This should only take a few seconds. Serve at once. Serves 4 as a meal or 6 as part of a Chinese dinner.

† No Added Salt.

BAKED "FRENCH FRIES"†

Try these baked fries if you want to avoid fried foods. These "fries" turn out crispy and crunchy.

4 medium-sized potatoes   **1 tablespoon oil**

Scrub the potatoes and cut into ¼ inch thick strips, ¼–½ inch wide and the length of the potato. Lightly oil two baking sheets and lay the potato strips down one at a time so they don't touch. Bake at 375°F. for 35–45 minutes, or until golden brown. If you prefer softer, thicker fries, cut them twice as thick, and bake as before. Salt to taste if desired, and serve at once. They lose their crispness if left to cool. Serves 4.

† Salt Free.

HASH BROWN POTATOES

A nice side dish with eggs, meat or beans.

4 medium potatoes   **1 teaspoon salt**
2 tablespoons minced fresh onion   **4 tablespoons butter**

Scrub the potatoes then cut into 1 inch thick slices. Steam for 18–20 minutes then chill in the refrigerator. Grate the cold potatoes and mix with the onion and salt. Melt the butter in a 10 inch skillet over medium heat then press the potato mixture into the pan allowing about ½ inch of space around the perimeter. Cook undisturbed for 10 minutes, or until the bottom has browned, then cut into 4 wedges and turn the pieces over. Brown the other side about 7 minutes, reducing the heat if necessary. Serve hot. Serves 4 generously.

SALAD†

Any mixture of raw vegetables is possible, but this salad combination is both delicious and attractive.

¼ head romaine
¼ head ruffled red lettuce
¼ pound spinach leaves
¼ pound cabbage
1 stalk broccoli
2 scallions

pint of cherry tomatoes
2 carrots
½ of a large cucumber
¼ pound fresh mushrooms
½ pound monterey jack or other cheese

Wash all the vegetables and shake the greens to remove excess moisture. Place in the refrigerator to chill. Remove the broccoli flowers and break into bite sized pieces. Cut the broccoli stalks into ¼ inch thick diagonal slices. Slice the tomatoes in half and thinly slice the carrots and cucumber. Cut the mushrooms vertically about ¼ inch thick and chop the cabbage and scallions. Grate the cheese, and refrigerate all ingredients in closed containers until just before serving. Now tear the romaine, lettuce and spinach into bite sized pieces and toss with the rest of the ingredients. Serve at once with salad dressing (see index) and croutons if desired. Serves 6–8.

VARIATION: • For a meal, add a sliced hard boiled egg on top of each serving along with additional cheese and strips of cold, cooked turkey or chicken.

† No Added Salt.

CROUTONS†

To garnish salads and soups.

whole wheat bread   **butter, softened**

Remove crusts from stale bread and butter lightly. Cut into ½ inch cubes or strips and bake in a preheated oven at 375°F. until golden brown. Allow to cool, then store in a tightly closed container.

VARIATIONS: • For garlic croutons, lightly sprinkle with garlic powder after buttering.
              • For onion croutons, lightly sprinkle with onion powder after buttering.

† No Added Salt.

VINAIGRETTE DRESSING

A lovely, mild dressing.

½ cup olive or safflower oil
3 tablespoons cider vinegar
1 tablespoon prepared Dijon mustard (don't substitute; its flavor is unique)

1 tablespoon minced fresh green onion
¼ teaspoon salt
⅛ teaspoon pepper
dash powdered garlic

Combine all ingredients in a small glass jar and shake well until mixed. Refrigerate until ready to use. Makes ¾ cup dressing.

ITALIAN DRESSING

A zesty, popular dressing.

1 cup safflower oil
6 tablespoons cider vinegar
1½ tablespoons dried parsley, crushed
¼ teaspoon crushed basil flakes

¼ teaspoon powdered oregano
¼ teaspoon pepper
1 teaspoon salt
½ teaspoon powdered garlic

Combine all the ingredients in a pint container and shake well. Refrigerate until ready to use. Flavor improves overnight. Makes 1⅔ cups dressing.

BLUE CHEESE DRESSING

Good strong blue cheese flavor, and oil-free!

3 ounces crumbled blue cheese
⅓ cup unflavored yogurt
⅓ cup skim milk
¼ cup nonfat dry milk powder
2 tablespoons cider vinegar

½ teaspoon salt
1 teaspoon dried parsley, crushed
⅛ teaspoon garlic powder
⅛ teaspoon dried minced onion

Combine all the ingredients in a blender or food processor and blend until smooth and creamy. You can add more blue cheese chunks if desired. Chill for several hours before serving to thicken the dressing as well as enhance its flavor. Store in the refrigerator in a glass jar or other tightly closed container. Makes 1 cup dressing.

MAYONNAISE

Easy to make, and preservative free!

1 egg
1 teaspoon honey
1 tablespoon lemon juice
1 tablespoon apple cider vinegar

1 teaspoon dry mustard
¾ teaspoon salt
⅛ teaspoon paprika
¾ cup safflower oil

Combine all the ingredients (except oil) in a blender until well mixed. With the blender on a low setting, begin pouring the oil into the mixture very slowly. If you add the oil too fast, the mixture will not thicken. Keep the blender going continuously as you mix the oil in. Continue blending for about 3 minutes until the mayonnaise is as thick as desired. Place in a tightly closed container and keep refrigerated. Makes approximately 2 cups.

CREAMY GARLIC DRESSING†

A favorite.

½ cup mayonnaise (see index)	1 teaspoon dried parsley, crushed
⅓ cup lowfat milk	¼ teaspoon powdered garlic
2 tablespoons unflavored yogurt	⅛ teaspoon pepper

Mix all the ingredients together and stir until well blended. Keep refrigerated. Makes about 1 cup.

VARIATION: • Add 1 tablespoon minced fresh onion or chopped chives.

† No Added Salt.

TARTAR SAUCE

The traditional accompaniment to fish.

Follow the basic Creamy Garlic Dressing recipe with the following changes. Mince a large garlic dill pickle and stir into the dressing. Makes about 1 cup.

TOMATO SAUCE

This thick, tasty sauce is basic to many of the recipes in this book. Use your garden tomatoes or buy tomatoes by the bushel in late summer for economy. You can freeze the sauce in pint containers so it will be easy to use whenever needed.

6½ quarts of quartered tomatoes
4 stalks chopped celery
3 onions, quartered
2 teaspoons garlic powder
1 tablespoon salt

2 tablespoons dried parsley, crushed
1 tablespoon oregano, crushed
2 teaspoons basil, crushed
¼ teaspoon pepper

Cook the tomatoes, onion and celery over low heat until the tomatoes soften and the mixture begins to liquify. Stir frequently. Then bring to a boil and turn back down and simmer for about one hour. Now ladle the mixture into a colander and catch the juice in a bowl. Stir the tomato mixture to remove the extra juice and ladle the thick tomato mixture into a blender. Blend until well mixed and then transfer to a sauce pan. Continue this process until all the cooked tomatoes have been used. The juice that has been saved in the bowl should be transferred into freezer containers to save for tomato juice drinks, soup beginnings or to use when cooking rice or stews.

Add the salt and spices to the tomato mixture in the sauce pan and heat to boiling. Turn down to simmer and cook another hour, or until thick. You will notice there was no mention of first scalding the tomatoes to remove the skins, or of seeding. The extra effort doesn't produce noticeably better results, and the important fiber is lost. Makes 6–7 pints sauce and about 8 pints juice.

PETE'S PICKLES

Strong, delicious garlic dills.

cucumbers, tiny or sliced in spears
pepper corns
red pepper, sliced
fresh dill springs
fresh garlic cloves

onion sliced (optional)
3 quarts water
1 quart apple cider vinegar
1 cup canning salt
½ teaspoon powdered alum

Select firm, unwaxed cucumbers of medium to tiny size. The best place to find unwaxed pickles is from a local gardener or vegetable market. Waxed cucumbers and peppers will not absorb the brine very well. If the cucumbers are small enough there is no need to slice them, but larger cucumbers should be cut into long spears about ¾ inch thick. Pack the cucumbers into quart size glass canning jars, leaving about an inch of space at the top. Now place 1 or 2 pepper corns in the jar, along with one slice of red pepper, 3 or 4, 2 inch pieces of fresh dill, and two small cloves of garlic. You may also add a slice of onion if desired.

Bring the water, vinegar, salt and alum to a boil in a large kettle. When the mixture is rapidly boiling, pour it over the cucumbers until all the vegetables are covered, allowing at least ¾ inch of space at the top of the jar. Make sure all the vegetables are covered with the brine, poking them down, or remove those that stick up. Wipe off the top of the jar so that it's clean and dry, then immediately seal. Place the sealed jars in a cool, dark place for 4–6 weeks before eating. Refrigerate after opening.

CRANBERRY RELISH†

Tart and delicious with turkey, chicken or pork.

1 pound raw cranberries
1 cup unsweetened apple juice
1 apple, finely chopped
¼ teaspoon ground ginger

⅔ cup honey
2 tablespoons lemon juice
1 tablespoon freshly grated orange peel

Bring all the ingredients to a boil in a small saucepan, and cook until the cranberries burst open. Turn down to simmer for 5 minutes then cool completely before serving. Refrigerate in a covered bowl. The mixture will gel when cold. Makes 3½ cups.

VARIATION: • You can substitute unsweetened orange juice for the apple juice. Add more honey to taste if necessary.

† Salt Free.

CHAPTER FIVE

Dried Foods

CHAPTER FIVE

Dried Foods

One of the oldest methods of preserving foods, dehydrating offers a simple and inexpensive method to store foods. Dried food requires much less storage space than freezing or canning since it has much less volume than the same food in its fresh state.

There are several methods of drying foods including the commercially manufactured dehydrator, your oven, a homemade dehydrator or the sun. Drying in the sun is only feasible in areas with low humidity, lots of sun and favorable breezes. However, sun-dried foods can lose up to 50% of their vitamin C content. Oven drying uses the most energy and takes much longer to effectively dry foods. Homemade dehydrators are suitable if you have the technical know-how to construct them. The fastest, most reliable and most efficient way to dry foods is with a commercial dehydrator. The initial purchase price is quickly recovered by the amount you can save in drying your foods. The longer it takes to dry foods, the more nutrients that are lost, therefore a commercial dehydrator retains the greatest amount of nutrients for your investment.

After years of dehydrating foods and trying various types of commercial dehydrators, the Harvest Maid ® FD-1000 dehydrator has proven to be a superior dehydrator and a sound investment. This model, with a round design and high speed fan, dries food very quickly and evenly, retaining the flavor and color of the original fresh fruit or vegetable.

Use the freshest, highest-quality foods possible for dehydrating to achieve good flavor and to assure high nutrition. As soon as the foods are washed and sliced, immediately begin dehydrating, don't let them sit on the counter. Foods with a high acid content should not be placed on metal trays. Keep individual pieces of food separate to allow for circulation and make sure they are of uniform thickness. You can test for dryness by cutting a piece in half and looking for any drops of moisture to appear. Properly dried foods will also feel dry, non-sticky and will lose the cool clammy texture. When the foods test dry, allow them to cool, test again, and then store in clean, tightly closed glass or plastic containers. Dried foods need to be kept in a cool, dark, dry place to avoid nutrient loss.

This chapter contains directions for drying a few of the foods that are commonly used in this book and how they can be used in lieu of fresh foods. Although fresh foods are generally preferable, the convenience and economy of dried foods make them an excellent alternative. Everyone enjoys dried fruits such as pineapple rings, apple rings and banana chips, and it is cheaper as well as tastier to dry

Harvest Maid® is a *registered trademark* of Alternative Pioneering Systems, Inc.

your own. Dried fruit is so much healthier than candy or other sweet treats, it's an ideal snack for children as well as adults.

It's possible to dehydrate almost anything, including meat, yogurt, eggs, ready-made soups, and every type of vegetable, fruit and herb. There are several excellent books devoted to dehydrating which are listed in the 'Recommended Reading' section of this book. These books provide any further information that you might require.

Please note, the times given for drying the various foods are based on the Harvest Maid® FD-1000. If you are using a different dehydrator, your time may vary widely. Expect oven drying, sun drying or a fan-less dehydrator to take much longer, up to 2–4 times longer. The amount of humidity in the air will also have an effect on drying time. People in arid regions will find it takes much less time to dry foods. Those who live near the Gulf of Mexico or other humid areas will have extended drying times.

Be sure to rotate the trays or sheets and turn the pieces of food over at least once, unless you have a dehydrator similar to the FD-1000 which makes these steps unnecessary. Small pieces of food such as herbs, chopped or minced vegetables should be stirred occasionally also. Follow the general instructions as well as specifics for each food listed.

When cooking with dried foods, add salt to the recipe after the vegetables have rehydrated and are plumped-up. Vegetables which have been steam blanched prior to drying will reconstitute more quickly. If the water or juice is rapidly absorbed when rehydrating fruits or vegetables, and the produce still looks shriveled, add more liquid until it will not absorb any more.

If dried fruits are drier and chewier than desired after being stored, you can plump them up by dipping the pieces in boiling water for about 15 seconds and then blotting the excess moisture on paper towels. Keep the plumped-up fruit in the refrigerator or use at once.

DRIED MUSHROOMS†

Select fresh, cultivated mushrooms and wash in cold water. Cut the bottom ¼ inch of the stem off and discard. Thinly slice (¼–⅛ inch) or chop the mushrooms uniformly and immediately place on the drying sheets. If desired, steam blanch for 5 minutes before drying. Allow space between each piece for proper air circulation. Start the dehydrator at 135°F. and dry them for 2 hours, then decrease the heat to 125°F. and continue drying for 1–3 hours depending on the thickness of the slices. The mushrooms are dry when they feel leathery, with no signs of moisture when cut in half. Also, pieces that are not quite dry tend to feel slightly colder when squeezed. When the mushrooms are dry, allow them to cool then store in an airtight container.

To use the mushrooms in the recipes, pour 1 cup of boiling water over 1 cup of dried mushrooms and allow 20 minutes for the mushrooms to absorb the water. Then simmer, stirring occasionally until most of the water is absorbed and the mushrooms are tender. Now measure according to the recipe as for cooked mushrooms. For use in soups, casseroles or main dishes you can add them directly with an equal addition of water. To add the dried mushrooms directly to a recipe, make sure the cooking time is 1 hour or longer.

† Salt Free.

DRIED TOMATO SLICES†

These are delicious as a snack or can be used in a variety of ways when cooking.

Choose firm, just-ripe tomatoes, wash and remove stem part. Slice ½ inch thick slices with an even thickness throughout (not like salad-sliced wedges). Place on plastic trays, not metallic because of the tomato's high acid content. Dry at 155°F. for 2 hours, then 125°F. for up to another 9 hours. They will be very thin and crisp when done. Check around the peel for any remaining moisture beads. When cool, store in airtight containers. They can be served as they are, topped with a slice of cheese for a tasty snack, or used in recipes.

For use in soups, break or cut the slices into quarters, then pour boiling water over them to cover and allow to rehydrate for 20 minutes, or put the pieces directly in the soup. Four to five slices equals a fresh tomato, depending on the size. You can also put the dried slices in the blender and make a fine tomato powder that can be used instead of tomato paste to thicken sauces and flavor recipes.

When a recipe calls for dried tomato pieces, simply break the dried slices into small pieces.

† Salt Free.

DRIED POTATO PIECES†

Another easy addition to soups and casseroles.

Select firm potatoes without any green areas on the skin and scrub well. Remove the eyes and any bruised areas, then chop into ½ inch cubes. If desired, steam blanch for 5 minutes before drying.* Dry at 155°F. for 2 hours, then 125°F. for about 4 hours more, possibly longer. They are dry when very hard, brittle and no moisture beads remain. When cool store in an airtight container. Dried potatoes lose their vitamin C quickly so they should be stored in a refrigerator or freezer. To use them in soup, simply stir in ⅓ cup dried pieces and ⅓ cup additional water in the soup for every medium potato called for in the recipe. You can also rehydrate them by pouring an equal amount of boiling water over them and allowing 20 minutes for them to absorb the water. Pour off the extra liquid before using, or simmer the potatoes in the liquid.

* Note: When dehydrating at temperatures below 120°F., always steam blanch the pieces for 5 minutes before drying them. This removes some vitamins, but will prevent the potatoes from turning black during the drying process.

† Salt Free.

DRIED MINCED ONIONS†

Wonderful flavor and ease of cooking in recipes.

First of all, dehydrating onions inside your house is not recommended. Set the dehydrator outside or everyone in the house will be suffering with watery eyes and noses. The odor is very strong. Select firm, unbruised onions, peel the outer skin off and cut off the ends. Chop or mince into small pieces. A food processor will save time as well as tears if you have many onions to dry. Dry the minced onions at 155°F. for 2 hours, then 125°F. for about 2 hours more. Since minced pieces cannot be easily spread out on the trays, stir the pieces at least once or twice while drying to "un-clump" them and faciliate even drying. When they are done they should be very hard and brittle. Cool, then store in a glass jar or other airtight container.

You can add dried onions directly to most any recipe with liquid in it. Use one-third to one-half as much dried onion as fresh called for in the recipe, depending on how "strong" the onions were that you dried. You can also put the dried pieces in the blender or grinder to make your own onion powder. Either way it's a convenient way to store onions and not have to risk spoilage. And you can get all the year's onion chopping done in one session!

† Salt Free.

DRIED CARROTS†

An easy food to dry, they offer the convenience of always being ready to add to soups or casseroles.

Scrub and trim fresh, firm carrots. You may either peel them or leave them intact. Thinly slice the carrots (⅛ to ¼ inch) or chop them into ⅜ inch pieces. If your method of dehydration is not a particularily fast one, steam blanch them for 5 minutes before drying. (It's really an option, so you can try them both with and without blanching to see which method you prefer.) Dry the pieces or slices at 155°F. for 2 hours, then 125°F. for about 4 hours more. They will be very tough or hard when done, with no moisture beads. After cooling, store in an airtight container. To preserve the vitamin A, dried carrots are best stored in the refrigerator or freezer.

The easiest way to use them in recipes is simply to stir the pieces into the hot liquid soup or casserole you are cooking. Make sure the cooking times allow for at least 1 hour for them to rehydrate. If the recipe calls for 2 large carrots, use ½ cup of dried slices. You can also cover them with an equal amount of boiling water, wait 20 minutes and then simmer until tender. The best taste comes from adding them directly to the soup, however.

Another option is to place the dried carrots in the blender to chop them into fine pieces for use in recipes or as flavoring.

† Salt Free.

DRIED CORN†

A favorite for drying and traditional in Pennsylvania Dutch recipes.

Select sweet, young, tender ears, remove the husk and trim. Steam blanch the cobs for about 2 minutes, or until the milk is set. Cut the kernels from the cob and dry at 155°F. for 2 hours, then 125°F. for another 5 hours or until crisp and brittle. The dried kernels should rattle when placed in a jar. Store the cooled, dried corn in an airtight container.

To use in recipes add ¼ cup of dried corn for every ½ cup of fresh corn called for and add an additional ¼ cup of water to the recipe. Another alternative is to cover the dried corn with an equal amount of boiling water and allow to sit for about 20 minutes. Pour off the excess water, if any, and then use. To serve as a vegetable for the table, soak the dried corn in an equal amount of milk for several hours in the refrigerator. Simmer the mixture for 30 minutes or until plump and tender. Season with butter and salt and pepper if desired.

Fresh cornmeal can be made by grinding the dried corn in a grain mill.

† Salt Free.

DRIED APPLES†

One of the most economical and delicious fruits to dry.

Any variety of apple may be dried, but tart apples, such as Winesap, Rome or McIntosh have the best flavor dried. Wash the apples, core and then peel if you have small children who might choke on the tough, somewhat crisp peels. Leave the peel on if you don't mind chewing a bit more. Cut the apples into slices or rings about ¼ inch thick. You may pre-treat them by dipping the slices in lemon juice before drying. Dry at 155°F. for 2 hours, then 125°F. for about 3 hours more. Test for dryness by removing a slice, allowing it to cool, then cutting it in half. No moisture beads should appear when squeezed. Pieces that aren't quite dry tend to feel cooler as well as moist. Remove the slices as they dry, allow to cool, then store in airtight containers. For a softer, chewier apple snack, reduce the drying time by about an hour. Since the apples will not be entirely dry, store in the refrigerator.

To rehydrate the apple slices for use in recipes, cover them with an equal amount of apple juice and place them in the refrigerator overnight. A faster method is to pour an equal amount of boiling apple juice or water over the slices. Wait 10–20 minutes, then pour off the liquid before using, or simmer the apples in the juice.

† Salt Free.

DRIED BANANA SLICES†

These are very sweet and chewy, not like the crisp fried banana chips available in stores.

Select ripe, unbruised bananas that are just beginning to get brown flecks on the peel. Slice the bananas about ⅛ to ¼ inch thick and dip in lemon juice or pineapple juice briefly to prevent discoloring. Dry at 155°F. for 2 hours, then 125°F. for up to 3–5 hours more. They will remain flexible, but should be dry and not overly sticky. Try folding a banana piece in half; if it sticks together, it's not dry enough. Allow the slices to cool, then store in a tightly closed container.

To rehydrate bananas cover with boiling water or fruit juice, depending on whether you object to the addition of another fruit's flavor to your recipe. Allow to sit for 20 minutes then drain off the remaining liquid and blend in the blender. You may need to add some of the drained liquid to get a smooth consistency. One cup of banana slices will reconstitute to about 1½ cups after the liquid has been returned, depending on how well you pack your measuring cup.

A variation when drying the slices is to sprinkle them with cinnamon or finely chopped nuts prior to drying. A delicious snack!

Note: For a toddler teething food, cut the bananas lengthwise, about ¼ inch thick, and dry in the long strips.

† Salt Free.

DRIED PEACHES†

Good for snacking or trail mix combinations.

Peaches should be very sweet, but not so ripe that they have become soft or have many bruised areas. Look for firm, undamaged peaches picked at the peak of the season. Cut into slices about ¼ inch thick and dip them in lemon juice or orange juice if desired, before drying. Dry the slices at 155°F. for 2 hours then 125°F. for about 5 hours more. Test for dryness by removing a slice, allowing it to cool, then cutting it in half. No moisture beads should appear when squeezed. Pieces that aren't quite dry tend to feel cooler as well as more damp. Remove the slices when dry, allow to cool, and store in airtight containers. For a softer, chewier peach snack, reduce the drying time by 1 hour. Since the peaches will not be entirely dry, they will need to be stored in the refrigerator or eaten at once.

To rehydrate the peach slices for use in recipes, cover them with an equal amount of water or fruit juice of your choice, and allow them to sit in the refrigerator overnight. A faster method is to pour an equal amount of boiling water or fruit juice over the peaches and let them sit for about 20 minutes. You can then pour off the excess liquid and use the slices, or simmer the peaches in the liquid until tender.

† Salt Free.

DRIED PEARS†

A favorite dried fruit.

Select sweet, firm, yet tender pears. Remove the skin or the dried fruit will have a gritty, sandy texture. Cut into ¼ inch slices and dip them in lemon or orange juice if desired. Dry the slices at 155°F. for 2 hours, then 125°F. for about 5 hours more. Test for dryness by removing a slice, allowing it to cool, then cutting it in half. No moisture beads should appear when squeezed. Pieces that aren't quite dry tend to feel cooler as well as moist. Remove the slices when dry, allow to cool and store in airtight containers. For a softer, chewier pear snack, reduce the drying time by 1 hour. Since the pears will not be entirely dry, they will need to be stored in the refrigerator or eaten at once.

To rehydrate the pear slices for use in recipes, cover them with an equal amount of water or fruit juice of your choice, and place them in the refrigerator overnight. A faster method is to pour an equal amount of boiling water or fruit juice over the pears and let them sit for about 20 minutes. You can then pour off the excess liquid and use the slices, or simmer the pears in the liquid until tender.

† Salt Free.

DRIED PINEAPPLE RINGS AND PIECES†

These take quite a long time to dry, but make a delicious chewy snack when finished.

Use a fresh, ripe pineapple, remove the outer rind and cut into ½ inch thick rings or pieces of even thickness. Dry for 2 hours at 155°F. then 125°F. for 12 to 15 hours more. Pineapple is done when it is still flexible, but not overly sticky and no moisture beads remain. Try pressing two pieces together; if they stick they aren't done. If you are using a slower method of drying, it may take up to 36 hours to dry the pineapple.

Note: Drying time can be reduced almost in half by slicing the pineapple to ¼ inch thick rings before drying; producing a very thin dried snack.

† Salt Free.

FRUIT LEATHER†

A very popular snack and much less expensive to make at home. Plus these are sugar and additive free.

Almost any combination of fruits or single fruit alone will make a delicious fruit leather snack, however, some favorites are listed below. Before you begin, make sure the fruits are clean, with any bruised or spoiled areas removed. Cut the fruit into about 1 inch chunks, and leave the peel on with the exception of bananas, pears, pineapple, watermelon, orange, etc. Puree the fruit in a blender or food processor until no large chunks remain. You can add up to 1 teaspoon lemon juice per cup of puree to help prevent darkening of the fruit.

Place the pureed fruit on lightly oiled plastic dehydrator sheets, or cover metal trays with plastic wrap that has been lightly coated with oil. Spread the puree out as evenly as possible, less than ¼ inch thick. Dry the fruit leather at 135°F. for 6–8 hours or until leathery and no longer sticky to the touch. Peel the leather off the trays and cut into serving size pieces if desired. Place on clean plastic wrap, and roll up jelly roll fashion to keep the leather from sticking to itself. Store the leathers in a plastic bag in a cool, dark place.

FRUIT LEATHER VARIATIONS:

- Apple Banana: 2 cups apple chunks, 2 cups banana chunks, ¼ cup orange juice.
- Pina-Colada: 2 cups pineapple chunks, 1 cup unsweetened coconut, ¼ cup pineapple juice
- Tropical: 1 cup pineapple chunks, 1 sectioned orange, 1 banana, ¼ cup unsweetened dried coconut, ¼ cup pineapple juice
- Strawberry Banana: 2 cups strawberries, 2 cups banana chunks
- Watermelon Apple: 2 cups watermelon, 2 cups apple chunks
- Apple Spice: 4 cups apple chunks, ¼ cup apple cider, 2 teaspoons cinnamon, ¼ teaspoon nutmeg
- Add up to 1 cup chopped nuts to any of the varieties.

† Salt Free.

Dried Apples, Dried Banana Slices and Dried Vegetables (Photo courtesy of Alternative Pioneering, Inc.)

DRIED HERBS, INCLUDING PARSLEY AND OREGANO†

There are two easy methods for drying herbs. You can simply put them in small brown paper bags with the stems tied together and hang each bunch upside down by its stems. Be sure to punch a few small holes in the bag for ventilation and hang the herbs in a warm airy location. It will take about 1 week to dry in this manner. The second method, drying herbs in a dehydrator, is much faster and preserves more of the flavor and essential oils. However, it's important that the temperature never rises above 110°F. First wash the leaves in cool water and remove the damaged leaves or stems. Spin or shake off the water, then allow to air dry briefly. If you are using the bag method, put the entire stem sections in the bag. If you are using a dehydrator you can dry the entire stem or the leaves only. Once the herb has dried it's easy to crumble the leaves away from the stem. Set the dehydrator at 100°F. and dry for 2–4 hours or until the leaves crumble easily and the stems are brittle. When dry and cool, store in airtight containers away from light.

Just before using the herbs in recipes, crush them in your fingers to release the full flavor.

† Salt Free.

CHAPTER SIX

Vegetarian Dishes

CHAPTER SIX

Vegetarian Dishes

For many people the term vegetarian conjures a picture of salads, beans, nuts and little else. In truth, lacto-ovo vegetarian meals, those containing milk and/or eggs, offer considerable variety and delicious high protein. There are many benefits for preparing meals without meat.

People become vegetarians for many reasons, both ethical and health-related. Many medical sources are now advising that we limit our meat intake. Dinners prepared without meat are generally much lower in saturated fat and cholesterol, even when milk products and eggs are included. Another benefit is that plant foods do not contain the level of pesticides often present in meats. Since pesticides and other contaminants are present in the food given to the animals, meat eaters receive the accumulated toxins.

The fear of not consuming enough protein is unwarranted if meals are well planned with an understanding of complementary proteins and amino acids. Very simply, there are eight essential amino acids which are needed in balanced proportions to maintain the human body. Plant foods all contain differing amounts of these amino acids, some being strong in one area, some in another. What is needed is to combine the foods so they complement each other and supply what is lacking. It's really quite easy. Milk products and eggs complement all plant proteins, but are especially beneficial with whole grains. Legumes (dried beans, lentils and garbanzos) combine well with seeds (sunflowers, sesame, etc.). Whole grains also go with legumes. That's all there is to it. A cheese sandwich is a complete protein, so are Bean Burritos. If in doubt, add a glass of milk or other milk product. There is a great deal of in-depth information on the subject, some source books are listed in the 'Recommended Reading' section.

Legumes contain roughly the same percentage of protein as meat does, and cheese is even higher. Soybeans top the list though, with over 40% protein. And the protein of all plant sources is increased when it is complemented as outlined above.

The following recipes contain many favorites such as Lasagna, Stuffed Peppers and Burritos. You are probably accustomed to preparing these with meat, but you will find that you will not miss the meat in these recipes, and neither will your family. If you are now serving meat every day, begin with one meat-less day a week using one of these recipes. As your family enjoys them, you can gradually add more. It might be wise, at first, to not mention that the Lasagna contains no meat until the meal is over. However you introduce these vegetarian recipes to your family, they are sure to enjoy them.

VEGETABLE QUICHE

An elegant dish to serve for guests.

2 tablespoons oil
¾ cup chopped onion
¼ cup chopped green pepper
1 cup chopped tomatoes
pinch of thyme
1 tablespoon dried parsley
½ teaspoon salt

4 eggs, beaten
1 cup milk
½ cup grated parmesan cheese
1 cup grated mozzarella (swiss cheese may be substituted for a more traditional, but higher-calorie quiche)

Sauté onions in oil until very soft and golden. Then add the green pepper, tomatoes and thyme. Cover and simmer 5 minutes then remove the lid and cook on low heat for about 15 minutes until the excess liquid has cooked away. Meanwhile prepare the Tomato Rye Pie Crust (see index). Mix together the parsley, salt, eggs and milk, then stir in the cheeses. When the vegetable mixture has cooled, add that to the cheese and milk, stir gently and pour into the prepared unbaked pie crust. Bake in a preheated oven at 350°F. for 40–50 minutes, or until a knife inserted in the center comes out clean. Delicious hot or cold with a salad and fresh bread. Serves 4–6.

LASAGNA

3 cups tomato sauce (see index)
½ teaspoon oregano, crushed
1 teaspoon basil, crushed
½ cup wheat germ
½ teaspoon garlic powder
1 pound ricotta *or* cottage cheese

2 tablespoons parsley, crushed
1 teaspoon salt
dash pepper
whole wheat lasagna noodles (see index)
½ pound mozzarella cheese, sliced
½ cup grated parmesan cheese

Heat tomato sauce in a small pan. If you do not have any sauce made according to the recipe in this book, please substitute 3 cups tomato sauce made without meat, as sold in natural food stores or supermarkets. Add the oregano, basil, wheat germ and garlic powder to the sauce and allow to simmer, uncovered. Mix together the ricotta, parsley, salt and pepper. Set aside while you bring a large pot of salted water (about ½ teaspoon salt) to a boil. Now place the lasagna noodles you made into the boiling water and cook about 12–15 minutes. Drain the noodles and preheat the oven to 375°F.

Butter a 9 × 13 inch baking dish and cover the bottom with one layer of noodles, add a layer of tomato sauce, then add a layer of the ricotta mixture. Next, add slices of mozzarella, then sprinkle with parmesan. Now repeat the procedure, beginning with the noodles, until all the ingredients are used and the cheese is on top. Sprinkle with additional parmesan and parsley if you like. Bake for 30 minutes. Serves 10.

VARIATION: • Steam one pound of fresh spinach until done and add to the tomato sauce mixture for more color, taste and nutrition.

STUFFED PEPPERS†

A beautiful dinner, but easy to make.

4 large green peppers
2½ cups cooked brown rice, cooled
8 ounces of mozzarella cheese, shredded
2 cups of tomato sauce (see index)

½ cup wheat germ
2 carrots, shredded
½ cup sliced mushrooms
parmesan cheese

Wash the peppers and slice off the top of each. Remove the seeds and core. Mix together the rice, cheese, tomato sauce, wheat germ, carrots and mushrooms. Fill each green pepper to the top with the mixture and sprinkle with parmesan cheese. Place in an oiled baking dish with about a ¼ inch of hot water on the bottom and bake in a preheated oven at 375°F. for 45 minutes or until tender. Serves 4.

† No Added Salt.

MACARONI AND CHEESE

A welcome change from the supermarket variety.

1½ cups uncooked whole wheat elbow
  noodles
¾ cup grated cheddar cheese
1 cup cottage cheese
¼ cup yogurt

½ cup grated parmesan cheese
1 egg, beaten
½ teaspoon salt
dash pepper
⅛ teaspoon garlic powder

Boil the noodles about 8–10 minutes until just cooked and still firm. Drain and rinse the noodles, then stir in ½ cup of the cheddar cheese and the rest of the ingredients and turn into a buttered 2 quart casserole dish. Sprinkle the remaining ¼ cup of cheddar on top and bake in a preheated oven at 300°F. for 50 minutes or until firm and golden brown on top. Serves 4.

PIZZA†

A nutritious complete meal everyone likes.

1½ teaspoons active dry yeast
½ cup warm (110°F.) water
1 tablespoon oil
1½ cups whole wheat flour
tomato sauce (see index)

½–¾ pound sliced mozzarella cheese
¼ cup grated parmesan cheese
toppings of chopped green pepper, sliced
  mushrooms, drained sauerkraut, black olives
  or sliced pineapple

Dissolve the yeast in the warm water, then stir in the oil. Slowly add the flour, a little at a time, while continuously stirring. When it becomes thick, turn onto a floured board and continue adding the flour, kneading it in by hand. Knead until smooth and elastic; it takes 7–10 minutes or so. Put the dough in a buttered bowl and cover with a damp cloth. Let it rise in a warm place until doubled, 40 minutes to 2 hours, depending on the temperature. For fastest rising, heat the oven to its lowest setting, turn it off, and place the dough inside after first letting most of the heat escape. After the dough has risen, punch down the dough and roll out to fit a 12 to 14 inch pizza pan. Oil the pizza pan, then place the dough on it, fluting the edges up slightly. If you want a thick crust pizza, let it rise again for 30–60 minutes in a warm place. For a thin crust, bake in a preheated oven at 400°F. for 8 minutes, then remove, cover with sauce, cheese and vegetable toppings. For the thick crust, bake and top as with the thin crust after the dough has risen that second time. Now put either version in the oven and continue baking for 5–10 minutes until the cheese is golden and the crust is lightly browned. Makes one 12 to 14 inch pizza.

† No Added Salt.

QUICK PIZZA

For pizza in a hurry, try this quick bread crust.

1½ cups whole wheat flour
½ teaspoon salt
2 teaspoons baking powder
½ cup water

2 tablespoons oil (optional)
tomato sauce (see index)
mozzarella
vegetable toppings

Mix dry ingredients then stir in water and oil. Roll out on a floured board and place on a lightly oiled 12 to 14 inch pizza pan. Bake in a preheated oven at 400°F. for 5 minutes, then remove, top with tomato sauce and sliced mozzarella cheese, along with your favorite toppings. Mushrooms, green peppers, olives and sauerkraut are favorites. Then put the pizza back in the oven for another 10 minutes, or until the cheese is golden. Makes one 12 to 14 inch pizza.

POTATO CHEESE CASSEROLE

This takes very little time to prepare and it smells so good when baking.

4 medium-sized potatoes
salt
pepper
garlic powder

onion powder
½ pound thinly sliced mozzarella
¼ cup grated parmesan cheese

Scrub and slice the potatoes thinly. Steam for 12 minutes or until tender. Butter a 1½ quart casserole dish and preheat the oven to 350°F. Layer about ⅓ of the potatoes on the bottom of the casserole dish and very lightly sprinkle with salt, pepper, garlic powder and onion powder. Cover with one layer of mozzarella slices, then sprinkle with parmesan. Add another layer of potatoes, spices and cheese. Repeat for the third time using the remaining cheese and potatoes. Now bake uncovered for 15 minutes. If golden-red cheese is desired (a favorite way), broil for one or two minutes before removing from the oven. Serves 4.

VARIATION: • Steam ½–1 cup of peas, lima beans or other green vegetable and layer with the potatoes.

BEAN BURRITOS

Fast and easy if you cook the beans and make the tortillas ahead of time.

2 tablespoons oil
1 medium chopped onion *or* **¼ cup dried minced onion**
3 cups cooked pinto beans
1 cup cooked rice (optional)
½ teaspoon garlic powder
2 tablespoons chili powder

1 teaspoon salt
½ teaspoon oregano, crushed
6 large tortillas (see index)
¾ pound grated cheddar cheese
2–3 chopped fresh tomatoes
½ head lettuce, torn into small pieces
1 small onion, chopped for table

Cook the onion in the oil in a medium sized skillet. When soft and golden, add the beans and mash most of them until thick. Then add the cup of cooked rice if you are including it, and the spices. The rice complements the protein in the beans and cheese, but it isn't essential for an "authentic" burrito. Cook the mixture on low heat for 30 minutes, stirring frequently. Serve on your home-made tortillas and top with grated cheddar, tomatoes, lettuce and onion. An entire well-balanced dinner that's fun, too! Makes 6 large burritos.

VARIATION: • Add sliced black olives, sour cream, salsa and/or sprouts when placing the cheese and other toppings on the tortillas.

VEGETARIAN STEW

Fast, easy and satisfying! Try with Sesame Crackers.

½ cup lentils
2 tablespoons oil
2 stalks celery, chopped
2 tablespoons dried minced onion
2 cups tomatoes, chopped
2½ cups water
½ cup barley

2 tablespoons tomato paste
1 teaspoon salt
dash pepper
pinch rosemary, crushed
¼ cup corn
½ cup carrots, grated

Sort through lentils to remove any foreign objects and rinse in cool water. Heat the oil and sauté the celery in a medium-sized sauce pan. When tender add the rest of the ingredients except the corn and carrots, and bring to a boil. Cover and simmer for 20 minutes, stirring occasionally, then add the corn and carrots and cook an additional 10 minutes with the cover on. Serve with crackers and cheese. Serves 4 with hearty appetites.

Note: If you choose to substitute dried vegetables for any of the fresh vegetables called for in the recipe, substitute the following amounts. Add all dried vegetables at the beginning and allow for an additional ½ hour of cooking time.

2 stalks celery . . . . ½ cup dried chopped celery plus ½ cup water
2 cups tomatoes . . . . 1 cup dried tomato pieces plus 1 cup water
¼ cup corn . . . . 2 tablespoons dried corn plus 2 tablespoons water

RICE

The basic accompaniment to Oriental dishes, as well as a hearty side dish topped with grated cheese.

2 cups brown rice
4¼ cups boiling water

1 teaspoon salt

Clean and wash the rice, rinsing carefully to drain off all the water. Stir the rice and salt into the boiling water and boil hard for 5 minutes, stirring and skimming off some of the foam that rises to the surface. Then cover tightly and turn down to simmer. Continue to simmer, without lifting the lid, for 45 minutes, then remove from heat and allow to sit, still covered for 5 minutes. Serve at once, the rice should be just perfect. Long grain rice is the best when cooking for the table. Short grain rice tends to be a bit sticky but is fine for soups. Serves 6.

BEANS

Just basic beans, to be used as a side dish or as a part of a complete meal when combined with cheese or other milk products and fresh vegetables. A touch of spice adds a zesty flavor.

2 cups dried pinto, navy or kidney beans
6 cups water
1 teaspoon salt

1 tablespoon dried minced onion
½ teaspoon chili powder
¼ teaspoon garlic powder

Wash and pick over the beans to remove any foreign material. Then bring the beans to a boil in just enough water to cover them. Now pour off the water, and add the 6 cups of water. Bring to a boil again, then turn down, cover and simmer for 3–4 hours, or until the beans are beginning to become tender. Now add the rest of the ingredients, mixing well, and continue to simmer for 1 to 2 hours more. Serve in a bowl with plenty of grated cheese on top, mozzarella is particularly good. For a complete meal, add a fresh salad, Corn Bread (see index) and cheese. Serves 6 as a side dish, 4 as a meal.

SANDWICHES†

Whole wheat bread with peanut butter topped with sliced banana.
Whole wheat bread with peanut butter topped with sliced apple.
Whole wheat bread with peanut butter topped with raisins or dates.
Pumpernickle bread with sauerkraut, swiss cheese, black olives, and mayonnaise (see index).
Pumpernickle bread with cream cheese, avocado slices, and alfalfa sprouts.
Pumpernickle bread with cream cheese, sliced black olives, and tomatoes.
Pumpernickle bread with swiss cheese and dill pickle.
Whole wheat bread with cream cheese and apple butter.
Whole wheat bread with cream cheese, raisins and cinnamon.
Spread tomato sauce on bread, top with mozarella cheese, and broil for an easy pizza.
Butter bread on outside, add your favorite cheese inside and grill.
Whole wheat bread with monterey jack cheese, sprouts and sliced tomato.
Mix hard boiled eggs with unflavored yogurt or mayonnaise (see index), minced onions and chopped celery and serve on whole wheat bread.
 The combinations are endless; hope this gets you started!

† Some Salt Free.

CHAPTER SEVEN

Meat, Poultry and Fish

Stir-Fried Chicken and Broccoli, Stir-Fried Pepper Steak and Rice

CHAPTER SEVEN

Meat, Poultry and Fish

It seems like there are a lot of "meat and potato" people in America, and even though recent medical reports urge the population to cut down on meat consumption, not everyone knows how to go about it. The following recipes use lean meats, but most of them also include an equal amount of whole grain and/or vegetable. This is one way to still serve meat, but get away from the large portions of meat so many eat every day.

When buying meat, always look for the leanest cuts available. When you get it home, remove *all* visible fat, as well as the skin from poultry. One exception is the roasting turkey, where the skin should be left on for cooking but removed prior to serving. Leaving the fat on the meat can double the caloric intake in many cases without providing much nutrition.

Another way to lower your fat intake is to blot browned meats on paper toweling before adding to the rest of the recipe or before serving. It simply removes the grease, nothing more. You'll be amazed at all the fat that is absorbed.

Some of the recipes in "Vegetarian Dishes" are also suitable for use with lean meats if you desire. For example a small amount (¼ to ½ pound) of browned hamburger could be added to the tomato sauce in the Lasagna recipe, or you could add nitrate-free meat toppings on the Pizza. But you'll find the vegetarian recipes are quite good as they are, and adding meat is not necessary.

You might want to start with one vegetarian day a week, to cut down your meat consumption, and gradually add more vegetarian dishes as your family enjoys them more. In any case, these recipes will provide you with delicious and healthful ways to serve meat.

CHICKEN AND RICE BAKE

This easy, yet terrific dish is perfect for guests.

1 chicken, cut into parts, with the skin and fat removed
1⅔ cups brown rice
3¼ cups water or stock left from cooking the mushrooms
⅔ cup cooked sliced mushrooms (drain liquid) (see variation)
¼ teaspoon powdered garlic

¼ cup yogurt
2 tablespoons whole wheat flour
1 tablespoon butter
2 tablespoons nonfat instant milk
1½ teaspoons salt
1 tablespoon dried parsley, crushed
1 teaspoon minced dried onion
dash pepper

Place the cut-up chicken in a 4 quart covered baking dish. Wash and clean the rice and put in the baking dish along with 2 cups of the water. Place the remaining water in the blender along with the mushrooms and remaining ingredients. Blend until smooth, then add to the chicken mixture. Stir well, then cover and bake in a preheated oven at 350°F. for 2 hours. Do not uncover the chicken until the baking time is over. Serve hot with steamed vegetables and a fresh salad. Serves 4–6.

VARIATION: • To use dried mushrooms instead of cooked, substitute ⅓ cup dried sliced mushrooms, cover with boiling water and allow to stand 15 minutes, then place the drained mushrooms in the blender and measure remaining water in with the stock.

CURRIED CHICKEN

A spicy Middle-Eastern dish.

1 whole chicken
2 tablespoons butter
2 teaspoons curry powder
1 medium apple, chopped
1 large onion, chopped
⅛ teaspoon ginger
1 cup chicken stock

½ cup dry milk powder
1 teaspoon salt
⅛ teaspoon pepper
⅛ teaspoon paprika
⅛ teaspoon cayenne pepper
2 tablespoons whole wheat flour

Place the chicken in 4 cups of water in a large pot and bring to a boil. Turn down the heat, cover and simmer for 1½ hours or until the chicken is well cooked and tender. Remove the chicken and take the meat off the bones, keeping the meat in large pieces if possible. Reserve the chicken stock in the kettle. Melt the butter in a large skillet and stir in the curry, cooking until brown. Add the apple, onion and ginger and cook for 5–8 minutes or until golden brown. Stir in the chicken stock, milk powder and spices. Heat to boiling. Stir in the flour to thicken and continue stirring until thick and bubbly. Turn off the heat, stir in the chicken pieces and serve at once over brown rice (see index). At the table include raisins, roasted peanuts, unsweetened coconut and chutney as condiments. Serves 4–6.

BARBEQUED CHICKEN

Serve this to your guests and everyone will want the recipe!

¼ cup tamari
½ cup tomato sauce (see index)
⅓ cup honey
2 tablespoons molasses
1 teaspoon vinegar
½ teaspoon powdered garlic

¼ teaspoon powdered dehydrated onion
½ teaspoon cinnamon
½ teaspoon ginger powder
1 teaspoon salt
¼ teaspoon ground pepper
4 pounds chicken, skin and visible fat removed

Mix all ingredients together except chicken. Stir in the chicken pieces and coat well. Place the mixture in the refrigerator and allow the chicken to marinate in the sauce for several hours. Bake the chicken in a preheated oven at 350°F. for 1 to 1¼ hours, basting with the extra sauce every 10–15 minutes. As an alternative you can broil or grill the chicken for about 15 minutes, then turn the pieces over and broil another 15 minutes. If grilled or broiled, the sauce tends to become black in places, but it still tastes good. Using the broiling method, you will need to baste the meat every 5 minutes. Serves 8 generously.

BARBEQUED SPARERIBS

Follow the basic Barbequed Chicken recipe but substitute 4 pounds of country style spareribs for chicken. Bake at 325°F. in a preheated oven for 2 hours, or until crisp. Broiling variation is the same as the chicken. Serves 8.

ROAST TURKEY

A Thanksgiving tradition as well as an economical meat any time.

If you purchase a frozen turkey, thaw it completely according to the directions on the wrapping. Remove the giblets. Rinse the turkey out with cool water, then sprinkle the inside cavities with salt, pepper and garlic and onion powder if you like. If you don't wish to stuff the turkey, place a large quartered onion and a chopped stalk of celery inside the large cavity for flavoring. Otherwise, loosely stuff the body and neck cavities with the Bread Stuffing (see index for recipe), and skewer or tie the cavities closed. Place the turkey breast side up in a large roasting pan. Covered black enamel pans are prefered because the turkey stays very moist and tender and cooks in a shorter period of time. An alternative method is to loosely cover the turkey with a tent of aluminum foil and baste with the drippings every hour or so. When the turkey is about ⅔ done, cut the string tying the legs together and continue roasting until done. The turkey is done when a meat thermometer inserted in the center of the thigh or breast registers 180°F. The drumsticks should move easily and feel very soft when pressed. Here is a time table for approximate roasting times. Cooking time will be somewhat shorter if you don't stuff the turkey, or if you use a covered black pan. Always bake in a preheated oven at 325°F.

6–8	pounds:	2½–3 hours		16–20 pounds:	5–6 hours
8–12	pounds:	3–4 hours		20–24 pounds:	6–7 hours
12–16	pounds:	4–5 hours			

Remove the turkey from the oven and allow it to sit for 15–30 minutes before carving. Scoop out the dressing, if used, and serve with cranberry relish, potatoes, and steamed green vegetables. If desired you can make a clear, broth-like gravy by simply pouring the turkey drippings from the pan into a bowl. Chill the bowl in the freezer for a few minutes until the fat rises to the top. Discard the fat, re-warm the broth and serve. For a thicker gravy add 1½ tablespoons whole wheat flour to a ½ cup broth and ½ cup water. Mix well and cook over low heat, stirring constantly, until thickened. You can add minced giblets and additional salt and pepper to taste, if desired.

VARIATION: • For salt free, omit sprinkling turkey with salt.

BREAD STUFFING

This is for a 6 to 8 pound turkey, double the recipe for a 12 to 16 pound turkey, triple it for a 20 to 24 pound turkey.

¼ cup melted butter
⅔ cup chopped onion
⅔ cup chopped celery
½ teaspoon thyme *or* sage, crushed
2 tablespoons dried parsley flakes

½ teaspoon salt
⅛ teaspoon ground pepper
6 cups whole wheat bread cubes *or* corn bread
  crumbs

Sauté the onion and celery in the butter for 5 minutes, then add the spices and herbs. Cook a few more minutes, then add to the bread and mix well. Do not stuff the turkey until just before roasting.

CRÊPES WITH TURKEY IN VELOUTÉ SAUCE

Very good, and easier than it sounds.

2 cups cooked, minced turkey
½ cup cooked mushrooms, chopped (see variation)
2 teaspoons minced dried onion
2 teaspoons salt
¼ teaspoon pepper

3 tablespoons butter
3 tablespoons whole wheat flour
2 cups vegetable or turkey stock
14 crêpes (see index)
¼ cup grated parmesan cheese

Combine the turkey, mushrooms, onion, 1 teaspoon salt and ¼ teaspoon pepper together and set aside. To make the veloute sauce, melt the butter in a small saucepan, remove from the heat and stir in the flour, mixing well. Cook for 1 minute over low heat, stirring constantly, then blend in the stock. Continue to cook over low heat, stirring until the sauce thickens somewhat. Stir in the remaining salt and a dash of pepper. Take ½ cup of the sauce and combine it with the turkey mixture, mixing well. Spoon about 2 tablespoons of the turkey mixture along the center of each crêpe, and roll into a cylindrical tube shape. Place each finished crêpe into a 9 × 13 inch baking dish that has been lightly buttered. When you have completed the crêpes, pour the remaining velouté sauce over the crêpes and sprinkle with the grated cheese. Bake in a preheated oven at 350°F. for 20 minutes, then turn the heat up and broil for about 3 minutes more, or until golden brown. Serve hot with a salad or steamed vegetable. Makes 14 filled crêpes, will serve 7.

VARIATIONS: • Substitute cooked chicken for the turkey.
• To use dried mushrooms instead of cooked, cover ¼ cup of dried sliced mushrooms with boiling water and allow to stand for 15 minutes. Then drain, chop the mushrooms and use as directed.

TURKEY POT PIE

Full of good things!

2 tablespoons butter
1 medium onion, chopped (see variation)
1 cup water
2 cups cooked, cubed turkey
1 cup peas, fresh or frozen
1 cup sliced carrots
1 cup green beans, fresh or frozen
½ cup fresh or frozen lima beans

2 teaspoons powdered vegetable broth
  seasoning (sold at natural food stores)
½ teaspoon salt
¼ teaspoon garlic
dash pepper
double whole wheat pie crust
1–2 tablespoons whole wheat flour

Sauté the onion in the butter until soft and golden. Add the water and bring to a boil, stirring in the turkey, vegetables and seasoning. Bring to a boil again, stir well, then cover and simmer for 20 minutes. Stir occasionally and add up to ¼ cup more water if necessary to keep the vegetables cooking and to prevent them from sticking. Meanwhile prepare a double recipe of the Basic Pie Crust (see index), placing one in a 9 inch pie plate and reserving the other crust for the top. When the vegetables are tender, stir in whole wheat flour one teaspoon at a time to thicken. The amount depends on how much liquid remains, so add it slowly, stirring well over low heat. Not more than 2 tablespoons should be necessary. Now spoon the mixture into the unbaked pie crust and cover with the second crust. Cut slits in the top in an attractive pattern. Bake in a preheated oven at 400°F. for about 20 minutes or until the crust is golden brown. Serves 4–6.

VARIATION: • To use dried onion instead of fresh, add ¼ cup dried minced onion directly to the water and bring to a boil. Stir in the butter along with the turkey and vegetables. Additional water may be needed to prevent the foods from sticking.

CHICKEN POT PIE

Follow the basic Turkey Pot Pie recipe but substitute 2 cups of cooked cubed chicken, preferably white meat, for the turkey.

STIR-FRIED CHICKEN AND BROCCOLI

Very attractive and delicious.

2 large chicken breasts, skin and bones
   removed
2 tablespoons whole wheat flour
1 tablespoon cider vinegar
1 egg white, beaten

1¼ teaspoons salt
1 stalk fresh broccoli
6 ounces fresh mushrooms
2 thin slices of peeled fresh ginger root
¼ cup peanut or safflower oil

Cut the chicken breasts into strips about ¼ inch thick and 2 inches long. Stir the flour into the chicken pieces until well mixed. Combine the vinegar, egg white and 1 teaspoon salt and add to the chicken mixture, stirring until mixed in. Now wash the broccoli, cut the flowers into serving-size pieces and cut the stalk into ¼ inch thick slices. Wash the mushrooms and slice ¼ inch thick also. Heat a wok or large skillet over high heat with 1 tablespoon oil until very hot (375°F.), but not smoking. Add the broccoli and stir-fry for 1 minute. Now add the mushrooms and ¼ teaspoon salt and stir-fry for another 2 minutes. Remove the vegetables from the wok to a serving bowl. Add the remaining 3 tablespoons of oil to the wok and heat to 375°F. again. Stir-fry the ginger slices for one minute then remove them. Add the chicken pieces and stir-fry in the hot oil for 4–6 minutes, or until they lose all traces of pink and are cooked through. The cooked vegetables should now be returned to the wok, stirring well. Remove from heat and place in a warmed serving bowl. Serve immediately with brown rice. Serves 4 as a main course or up to 8 as part of a Chinese meal.

VARIATION: • Substitute 6 ounces fresh snow peas or sugar snap peas for the broccoli, but stir-fry 2 minutes instead of 3 minutes. Simply add the peas, mushrooms and salt at once.

SWEET AND SOUR PORK

A favorite Chinese dish.

1 pound lean, boneless pork
5 tablespoons whole wheat flour
4 tablespoons cornstarch
½ cup vegetable stock (use water left from steaming vegetables)
1 teaspoon salt
1 egg, beaten
2 cups peanut or safflower oil
1 green pepper, seeded and cut into ½ inch pieces

1 carrot, cut into ¼ inch wide strips, 2 inches long
1 clove minced fresh garlic
¼ cup pineapple juice
3 tablespoons honey
4 tablespoons apple cider vinegar
2 teaspoons tamari
¼ cup crushed unsweetened pineapple, drained
2 tablespoons cold water

Remove visible fat from the pork and cut into 1 inch cubes. Mix the egg, flour, 3 tablespoons of the cornstarch, salt and ¼ cup of the vegetable stock together in a medium sized bowl. Place the 2 cups of oil in a wok or large skillet and heat to 375°F. over high heat. Watch the temperature carefully to keep the oil from smoking. Place half the pork in the flour batter, stir well and drop the pieces one by one into the hot oil. Stir gently, watch the temperature and cook for 6–8 minutes or until golden brown. Remove from the wok, drain on paper towels and place in a preheated oven at 300°F. Now coat the rest of the pork and cook in the same way. Once the pork is done and in the oven, drain the oil from the wok and return only one tablespoon of oil. Turn the heat on high for about 1 minute, then stir in the green pepper, garlic and carrots. Stir-fry for 3 minutes, being careful that the mixture doesn't burn. Now stir in the pineapple juice, remaining vegetable stock, honey, vinegar, tamari and crushed pineapple, and bring to a boil. Cook for about 1 minute, then stir in the 1 tablespoon cornstarch dissolved in the 2 tablespoons cold water. Cook another 15 seconds, stirring continuously, until the sauce is thickened, then pour over the fried pork pieces and serve at once. This dish should be served with cooked Brown Rice (see index) and fresh Steamed Broccoli or Stir Fried Vegetables (see index). As part of a Chinese meal for guests you should also consider making at least one or two other Oriental dishes for variety. At a traditional Chinese meal, several entrees are presented along with individual bowls of rice and everyone is free to sample some of each. It's a lot more fun that way, too. Don't forget to serve tea, and fresh fruit for dessert. Serves 4 as a main course or up to 8 as part of a Chinese meal.

STIR-FRIED PEPPER STEAK†

A favorite family dinner.

1 pound lean beef
3 tablespoons tamari
1 tablespoon apple cider *or* other fruit juice
½ teaspoon honey
1 tablespoon whole wheat flour

1 large carrot
1 large green pepper
⅛ teaspoon ginger powder
¼ cup oil

Cut the beef into 2 inch long strips, about ½ inch thick, removing all fat and gristle. Mix the tamari, apple cider, honey and flour in a bowl and then stir in the beef. Mix well. Allow to marinate for several hours if possible. Cut the carrots and green peppers into 2 inch long strips and ¼ inch wide.

Heat 1 tablespoon of oil in a wok or large skillet and heat to 375°F. but not smoking. Stir-fry the carrots and green pepper for about 3–5 minutes, or until tender but not soft. Remove the vegetables with a spoon and place on a serving plate. Place the rest of the oil in the wok or skillet and heat to 375°F. Stir in the ginger, then the beef strips and stir-fry for about 3–4 minutes, or until cooked through. Stir the vegetables into the beef, and stir-fry for 1 minute, then place the entire mixture on a serving platter and serve over brown rice (see index). Serves 4 as a main course, or up to 8 as part of a Chinese meal.

† No Added Salt.

EGG ROLLS

Include these for a delicious dinner on a special occasion.

8 ounces lean pork
2 chicken breasts (bones and skin removed)
2½ cups safflower or peanut oil
⅔ cup thinly sliced fresh mushrooms
1 tablespoon tamari
1 tablespoon apple cider
½ teaspoon honey
2 cups thinly sliced celery

1 cup thinly sliced water chestnuts
1 cup fresh bean sprouts
2 teaspoons salt
1 tablespoon cornstarch
2 tablespoons vegetable stock
1 package whole wheat egg roll wrappers sold in natural food stores
1 egg, beaten

Chop the pork into small pieces about ½ inch thick. Chop the chicken into ½ inch thick pieces and set aside. Heat 1 tablespoon of the oil in a large skillet or wok and stir-fry the pork pieces until the pink color is gone, or about 2 minutes over medium-high heat. Stir in the chicken pieces and mushrooms and continue to stir-fry until the chicken loses it's pink color. Add the tamari, apple cider and honey and stir-fry for 1 more minute, then place the mixture in a bowl.

Place 2 additional tablespoons of oil in the skillet or wok and heat to medium high. Stir-fry the celery and water chestnuts for 5 minutes, then add the bean sprouts and salt and stir-fry for an additional minute. Now add the meat mixture and stir until well mixed. Dissolve the cornstarch in the vegetable stock and stir into the mixture until the liquid contents have thickened. Remove from the heat and allow to cool to room temperature.

Place about ⅓ cup of the cooled mixture diagonally on the center of an uncooked egg roll wrapper, and fold envelope side. Bottom triangle up, sides in, then the top down, sealing it with brushed-on raw egg. If you can't cook the egg rolls immediately, cover with plastic wrap and refrigerate.

Heat the 2¼ cups remaining oil in a large skillet or wok over medium-high heat until very hot, but not smoking. Place 5 egg rolls in the hot oil and cook them for about 2–3 minutes per side, turning them over when they are golden brown. Remove with a slotted spoon and place on paper toweling. Fry the remaining egg rolls in this manner and serve at once. These can be kept warm for up to an hour in a preheated oven at 250° F., but they will lose some crispness. Egg rolls can be rewarmed in a preheated oven at 400° F. for about 12 minutes. Makes 15 large egg rolls. Will serve 4 as a main course, or 8 as part of a Chinese meal.

ORIENTAL LIVER†

A tasty way to enjoy liver. Especially good with a salad and potato.

12 ounces liver, cubed
2 tablespoons tamari
6 tablespoons water

4 teaspoons dried minced onion
½ teaspoon powdered garlic

Combine all ingredients in a medium skillet and cook covered on medium low heat, stirring frequently. Remove from the heat when cooked all the way through. Cooking time is about 10 minutes depending on the size of the liver pieces. Serves 4.

† No Added Salt.

BEEF STROGANOFF

A special dinner anytime.

3 tablespoons butter
1 pound lean beef cut into ½ inch strips, 1½ inches long with all the fat trimmed away
1 tablespoon whole wheat flour
½ teaspoon salt
⅛ teaspoon pepper
½ cup cooked mushrooms, drained (see variation)

1 tablespoon dried minced onion
2 teaspoons dried parsley flakes
⅛ teaspoon garlic powder
1½ cups vegetable stock (use water from mushrooms)
2 cups whole wheat egg noodles (uncooked)
1 cup sour cream

Melt 2 tablespoons of the butter in a large skillet over medium heat. Combine the meat, flour, salt and pepper, mixing well. Brown the meat in the butter, stirring to cook evenly. When nicely brown, stir in the mushrooms, onion, parsley, garlic and vegetable stock. Bring to a boil, then turn the heat down to low and cook uncovered for 1 hour or until the mixture is thickened. In a large sauce pan cook the noodles in boiling, salted water for 8–10 minutes or until firm but tender. Drain off the water and stir in the remaining tablespoon of butter. Stir the sour cream into the beef mixture, and serve at once over the noodles. A fresh green salad is excellent with this. Serves 4–6.

VARIATION: • To use dried mushrooms instead of cooked, substitute ¼ cup dried sliced mushrooms, cover with boiling water and allow to stand 15 minutes, then add the drained mushrooms to the meat mixture and measure remaining water in with the vegetable stock.

SAVORY BEAN CASSEROLE

Hearty and delicious, with a barbeque tang.

1 pound lean ground beef
1 large onion, chopped *or* ¼ cup dried minced onion
2 cups cooked kidney beans
2 cups cooked garbanzos
2 cups cooked navy beans
2 cups fresh or frozen lima beans
1½ tablespoons molasses

1½ tablespoons honey
1½ tablespoons prepared mustard
½ cup tomato sauce (see index)
3 tablespoons apple cider vinegar
1 teaspoon ground cumin
¼ teaspoon dried minced garlic
1 teaspoon salt
¼ teaspoon pepper

In a large kettle, brown the ground beef and cook the onion. Drain off the grease then stir in the rest of the ingredients. Bring to a boil, stirring frequently, then cover and simmer for 1 hour. Serve with Corn Bread or Cheese Crackers (see index). Serves 6.

RISOTTO

A family favorite.

½ pound ground lean hamburger
1 small onion
¼ teaspoon garlic powder
3 cups unsalted tomato juice (see index) *or*
  ⅓ cup tomato paste and 2 ⅔ cups water
¾ teaspoon oregano, crushed

1 teaspoon dried parsley, crushed
pinch celery seed
¼ teaspoon basil, crushed
1½ teaspoons salt
1 cup brown rice, cleaned and rinsed in cool
  water

Brown the hamburger with the onion, then drain and place on paper towels to absorb excess fat. In a medium sized pan, bring the tomato juice (or water and tomato paste combination) to a boil. Stir in the meat and onion mixture, spices and the rice. Allow to boil a minute, turn down to simmer, and cover. Cook for about 50 minutes, stirring occasionally, until the liquid is absorbed. Serve with parmesan cheese on top. Serves 4.

VARIATION: • Use only ¼ pound hamburger and add ¼ pound sliced mushrooms.

POTATO SKILLET DINNER

This is easy and with it you don't have to cook a side dish.

½ pound lean hamburger
2 tablespoons dried minced onion
⅔ cup water
4 medium potatoes, sliced
2 teaspoons dried parsley

1 teaspoon salt
¼ teaspoon garlic powder
¼ teaspoon ground pepper
½ cup fresh or frozen peas

Brown the hamburger with the onion and drain off the oil. Then add the water, parsley, potatoes and spices and bring to a boil. Turn down to simmer and cover, stirring frequently to keep the potatoes from sticking. You can add more water if necessary. Cook for 10–15 minutes or until the potatoes just begin to become tender. Then stir in the peas and cook another 6–8 minutes, still covered, and stir occasionally to keep from sticking. A meal by itself, but nice with corn on the cob or a salad. Serves 3–4.

VARIATION: • Substitute green beans or other vegetables for the peas.

GOULASH

A childhood favorite.

½ pound lean hamburger
1 tablespoon dried minced onions
2 cups tomato sauce (see index)

1 teaspoon salt
2 cups whole wheat ABC or elbow noodles
parmesan cheese

Brown the hamburger with the onions and then drain off the grease. Remove the hamburger and onion from the pan and place on paper towels to absorb more of the fat, then return to the skillet. Now add the tomato sauce and salt and cook over low heat until the sauce bubbles. Allow the sauce to simmer gently while you start a large kettle of water boiling for the noodles. When the water reaches boiling, stir in the noodles and gently boil for 8 to 10 minutes, or until the noodles are just tender but still firm. Drain the noodles and mix the noodles and sauce together. Serve immediately with plenty of grated parmesan cheese to top each serving. Steamed broccoli is a nice accompaniment, or choose your favorite green vegetable. Serves 4.

VARIATION: • Add ⅓ cup chopped green pepper when browning the hamburger and onions.

GYROS

A delicious Greek sandwich.

1 pound ground lamb *or* hamburger
1 slice whole wheat bread, toasted and
  crumbled in blender
¼ cup chopped fresh onion *or* 2 tablespoons
  dried minced onion
½ teaspoon salt

¼ teaspoon pepper
½ teaspoon allspice
¼ teaspoon dried minced garlic
½ teaspoon coriander
¼ teaspoon dried savory, crushed

Combine all the ingredients and brown in a large skillet. When done serve in whole wheat Pita Bread (see index) with sliced tomatoes marinated in Italian Dressing (see index), fresh parsley and unflavored yogurt. Serves 4–6.

VARIATION: • Add sliced black olives and slices of feta cheese when assembling the sandwich.

SLOPPY JOES

The kids all love these!

1 pound lean hamburger
4 teaspoons dried minced onion
1 ⅓ cups tomato sauce (see index)
1 cup cooked pinto beans

½ teaspoon salt
¼ teaspoon garlic powder
⅛ teaspoon chili powder

Cook the hamburger and onion together over medium-low heat until well done. Drain off the liquid and blot dry on paper toweling. Return the hamburger and onion to the skillet then add the rest of the ingredients, mixing well. Heat to a boil, then turn down and simmer for 30 minutes. Serve on toasted whole wheat English Muffins, Whole Wheat Bread, or whole wheat Pita Bread (see index for recipes). Excellent in pita pockets with a fresh green salad and steamed corn on the cob, but Baked "French Fries" and steamed vegetables are a tasty accompaniment too. Serves 6.

VARIATION: • Top each sandwich with a slice of cheddar and broil for 1 minute in the oven to melt the cheese.

BROILED FISH

A delicious way to enjoy fish.

2 pounds of cleaned, halved perch, trout or
other fresh fish
2 tablespoons butter

salt
pepper

Heat the oven to broiling. Lightly sprinkle the fish with salt and pepper and place skin side down on a broiler pan. Dot the fish with butter and broil 2 inches below heat for about 5–10 minutes or until golden brown. Turn the fish and brown the other side for about 5 minutes longer. Serve with additional butter, lemon and fresh parsley sprigs. Serves 4.

VARIATION: • For salt free, omit salt.

CRISPY BAKED FISH

You can make your own fish fillet sandwich or eat as an entree.

1½ pounds white fish fillets, perch, cod, whitefish, etc.
1 slice whole wheat bread
¼ cup whole wheat flour
¼ cup cornmeal

¾ teaspoon salt
1 teaspoon baking powder
2 tablespoons butter
1 egg, beaten

Buy fresh or frozen fillets and cut into 4-ounce serving-size pieces. Combine the bread, flour, cornmeal, salt and baking powder in a food processor or blender and blend until fine. Add the butter and blend again until well mixed. Place this mixture on a plate and place the beaten egg in a shallow bowl. Wash the fish and pat dry with paper toweling. Next dip the fish in the egg and then in the flour mixture, coating all sides well. Place on a lightly oiled baking pan. Bake in a preheated oven at 375°F. for 30 minutes, turning once at 15 minutes. Both sides should be crispy. Serve hot with Baked French Fries (see index) and a vegetable. Serves 6.

FISH SANDWICH

Follow the Crispy Baked Fish recipe, but just before removing from the oven, place a slice of monterey jack cheese on each, wait 1 minute, then remove from oven and serve in whole wheat bread. Serves 6.

TUNA FISH HOTDISH

A nice family dinner.

⅔ cup cooked mushrooms (see variation)
⅓ cup vegetable stock, *or* water from cooking
  mushrooms
¼ cup unflavored yogurt
2 tablespoons whole wheat flour
2 tablespoons nonfat dry milk
1 tablespoon butter
1 teaspoon salt

1 teaspoon dried minced onion
⅛ teaspoon garlic powder
1 tablespoon dried parsley, crushed
dash pepper
2 cups uncooked whole wheat elbow macaroni
2 6½ ounce cans water-packed tuna, drained
6 whole wheat crackers

Place the mushrooms, vegetable stock, yogurt, flour, milk, butter, and spices in the blender or food processor and blend until smooth. Cook the noodles in boiling water 8–10 minutes or until tender but still firm. Drain the noodles and mix with the tuna and mushroom mixture, stirring well. Spoon into a buttered 2½ quart casserole dish. Crumble the crackers and sprinkle over the top. Bake in a preheated oven at 325°F. for 20–30 minutes or until the top is lightly browned and somewhat crispy. Serve hot with fresh green vegetables. Serves 4–6.

VARIATION: • To use dried mushrooms instead of cooked, substitute ⅓ cup dried sliced mushrooms, cover with boiling water and allow to stand 15 minutes, then place the drained mushrooms in the blender and measure remaining water in with the vegetable stock.

TODDLER MEATS†

Easy to do and very economical.

When you are preparing meat for the rest of the family, select a ¼ pound portion and keep it seperate from the rest of the meat. Choose a very lean piece and bake it in a separate dish, covered with foil. This works well with chicken, turkey, beef and pork. The cooking time will be about 30–40 minutes or slightly more, so check for doneness. You can also brown a piece of meat seperately on the range, but it will not be as tender as baked meat. When the meat is cooked through without any traces of pink, allow to cool slightly, then grind in a blender, meat grinder or baby food mill. Make sure no gristle or fat is on the meat before grinding. You may need to add a little water to achieve the right consistency, but do not add salt or any other seasoning.

    Once ground, the meat may be fed to the child immediately, or you can freeze it in an ice cube tray for use later. Just remove one or two cubes and warm at serving time.

† Salt Free.

CHAPTER EIGHT

Snacks and Crackers

CHAPTER EIGHT

Snacks and Crackers

Today's supermarket aisles are lined with a dazzling array of snacks and crackers that Americans consume with a voracious appetite. Unfortunately, most of the products are highly salted, loaded with oil or animal fat and made with refined flours. There has been improvement, however, and many snacks are now available without preservatives and other artifical ingredients. Many crackers also contain some whole-grain ingredients and a few are cutting down on the salt. But it is still very difficult to find a completely whole-grain cracker or snack unless you shop at a natural food store.

The good news is that all the recipes in this chapter are simple to make, and very inexpensive. A child can mix up the snack recipes, while the cracker recipes involve only a little more effort. What is most impressive, however, is that these snacks and crackers are good for you, as very small amounts of salt and oil are used, or none at all.

They are ideal to take traveling, hiking, bicycling or in lunch boxes, as well as being great for an occasional handful between meals. Served with milk, cheese or yogurt, these snacks and crackers can provide a protein-rich mini-meal when you don't have time for more. When traveling, take a large container of a nut and dried fruit mix, as well as whole-grain crackers. Then you can simply stop at a market and buy some cheese or yogurt and a cold container of fruit juice to enjoy with the crackers and mix. It's a good feeling to know that when you travel you can still eat nutritiously even though you don't want to take the time to stop at a restaurant.

Of course, some of the best snacks come already made: raw fruit, vegetables, nuts and nut butters, seeds, dried fruits, vegetables, fruit leather, cheeses and yogurt. Refer to Chapter Five for dried food snacks. To encourage your family to eat healthier snacks, simply keep a good supply of fresh fruit and vegetables washed in pretty bowls in the front section of your refrigerator or on the table. Put the nuts, seeds and dried fruit in clear glass jars in the refrigerator door where they can be easily seen, and leave the cheeses and peanut butter next to the fruit and vegetables. Hide the more fattening foods in the back, where they are difficult to see and hard to reach. It's a simple thing to do, but it really works. Children will even reach for a celery stick or carrot or green pepper slice if they are fresh, already washed and easy to find. When children are "starving!" an hour before dinner, let them eat all the raw vegetables they want, along with a small chunk of cheese or a handful of nuts. That way, if they don't finish their dinner, you know what they did eat was good for them.

CHEESE CRACKERS

These are so good you have to make a double batch to make them last more than an hour!

1¼ cups whole wheat flour
¼ teaspoon salt
⅛ teaspoon paprika
⅛ teaspoon garlic powder
3½ tablespoons butter

¼ cup grated parmesan cheese
1 cup finely grated sharp cheddar, (undyed) or other sharp cheese
1 egg yolk, beaten
2 tablespoons water

Combine the flour, salt and spices, then cut in the butter and cheeses. A food processor makes this easier. When well blended, add the egg yolk and water, stir and form into a soft dough ball. If necessary add another teaspoon of water until it sticks together, but not too much, because the dough should remain slightly crumbly. Roll out thinly and cut into small squares about 1½ inches across. You can also cut the dough into other shapes, but be sure they are of even thickness to ensure even baking. Now place on ungreased baking sheets and prick the tops with a fork. Bake in a preheated oven at 350°F. for 15–20 minutes or until golden brown. Cool on a wire rack and store in a tightly closed container. Makes 3–4 dozen crackers.

SESAME CRACKERS

Homemade crackers are so easy to make and so much better tasting, not to mention cheaper, than store bought, you'll wonder why you never tried them before!

3 cups whole wheat flour
1 cup cornmeal
1 teaspoon salt

½ cup unrefined corn oil
up to 1 cup buttermilk
sesame seeds

Mix flours and salt. Stir in oil and gradually add the buttermilk until the dough holds together but is soft enough to roll. Knead lightly. Roll out on a lightly floured surface until about ⅛ to ¼ inch thick, depending on how crisp you like your crackers. Thicker crackers will be chewy, but not as crisp. Sprinkle liberally with the sesame seeds and lightly roll them into the dough to press them into the surface. Cut into squares. Bake on a cookie sheet in a preheated oven at 375°F. for about 20 minutes, or until brown. Pricking the surface of the crackers before baking will help keep them flat.

VARIATION: • Omit salt for salt free.

RYE CRACKERS

2 cups rye flour
2 cups whole wheat flour
2 teaspoons salt

⅓ cup unrefined corn oil
1 cup buttermilk

Follow the same directions as given for Sesame Crackers, with the following exceptions: roll the crackers very thinly, from ¹⁄₁₆ to ⅛ inch, cut into squares or rectangles and bake in a preheated oven at 400°F. for 10 minutes after first pricking the tops of the crackers with a fork.

VARIATION: • Omit salt for salt free.

GRAHAM CRACKERS

Loved by both young and old.

2⅓ cups whole wheat flour
1½ teaspoons baking powder
½ teaspoon salt
¼ cup milk powder

¼ teaspoon cinnamon
½ cup soft butter
⅓ cup honey
⅓ cup milk

Combine the dry ingredients, then cut in the butter until well mixed and crumbly. Stir in the honey and milk and work with your hands to make a stiff but smooth dough. Roll out on a floured board to a thickness of ⅛ to ¼ inch thick. The thinner cracker is crisper, like store-bought, and the thicker one is more like a cookie. Cut into squares or rectangles and place on ungreased cookie sheets. Prick the tops with a fork and brush lightly with milk. Bake in a preheated oven at 400°F. for 8–10 minutes for thin crackers and about 15–18 minutes for thicker ones. Cool on wire racks, then store in a tightly closed container.

VARIATION: • Omit salt for salt free crackers.

TODDLER TEETHING CRACKERS†

Simple and not nearly as messy as many commercial teething crackers.

Use slices of the Whole Wheat Bread recipe (see index), making the bread without milk or honey (substitute orange juice concentrate or molasses for the honey). Remove the crust, and cut the slices into about ½ inch wide strips the length of the slice. Place the bread strips on an ungreased cookie sheet and bake in a preheated oven at 250°F. until totally dried out. This will take about an hour. Store the strips in an airtight container to keep them hard and dry.

† No Added Salt.

FRESH ONION DIP†

Terrific with crackers or preservative-free potato chips.

8 ounces cream cheese
¼ cup skim milk

2 tablespoons fresh minced onion
2 teaspoons dried parsley flakes

Blend all ingredients together until smooth. Keep refrigerated in a closed container until ready to serve. Makes 1½ cups dip.

† No Added Salt.

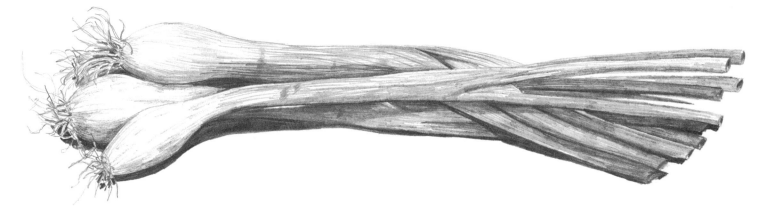

BLUE CHEESE DIP†

This is good with both raw vegetables and crackers or potato chips.

8 ounces cream cheese
4 ounces blue cheese, crumbled

¼ cup skim milk
2 tablespoons dried parsley flakes

Blend all ingredients together until creamy but still slightly lumpy from the blue cheese pieces. Keep refrigerated in a closed container until ready to serve. Makes 2 cups dip.

† No Added Salt.

FRUIT DIP†

Delicious for dipping apple and pear slices in, as well as other fruits and vegetables.

4 ounces cream cheese
¼ cup unflavored yogurt

3 tablespoons orange juice concentrate

Combine all the ingredients and mix well. Keep refrigerated. Makes about 1 cup dip.

VARIATIONS: • Stir in ¼ cup crushed pineapple after mixing the cream cheese with the yogurt and orange juice.
• Stir in ¼ cup chopped nuts.

† No Added Salt.

TRAIL MIX†

A healthy snack for skiing, hiking or anytime.

1 cup roasted, unsalted peanuts
1 cup raw almonds, unblanched
½ cup raw cashews
½ cup dried coconut flakes

1 cup raisins
½ cup dried pineapple chunks
½ cup dried apple slices
½ cup dried date pieces

Mix all the ingredients together and store in a tightly closed container. Refrigerate if keeping for a long period of time. Makes 5½ cups.

VARIATION: • Substitute walnuts, pecans, sunflower seeds, filberts or any other raw nut or seed for the ones listed. Or add them all together!

† Salt Free.

CAROB DELIGHT†

A sweet treat to please everyone.

1 cup carob chips
1 cup peanuts, roasted unsalted
½ cup dried coconut flakes

1 cup raisins
½ cup almonds, raw unblanched

Mix all the ingredients together and store in a tightly closed container. Refrigerate if keeping for a long period of time. Makes 4 cups.

† Salt Free.

CHEESY POPCORN†

A tasty variation from buttered, and nutritious as well.

Pop the corn in a hot air popcorn popper and pour into a large roasting pan, or other large, shallow pan. Sprinkle generously with parmesan or grated cheddar cheese, and bake in an oven at 350°F. until the cheese melts. Serve at once.

† No Added Salt.

SUNFLOWER SEED SNACK†

This is so good you can hardly stop eating them!

3 cups hulled raw sunflower seeds   **¼ cup tamari**

Mix together the sunflower seeds and tamari and turn into a 9 × 13 inch baking pan. Bake at 325°F. in a preheated oven for about 25 minutes, stirring every 7 minutes. Seeds are done when dry and golden brown. Allow to cool and store in a tightly closed container. Makes 3 cups.

† No Added Salt.

CHAPTER NINE

Desserts

CHAPTER NINE

Desserts

Most everyone looks forward to dessert, but most sweets offer little food value except as calories. Many box mixes, refrigerated doughs and frozen desserts are loaded with additives, preservatives, refined flours and sugars. Chocolate, common in many dessert offerings, poses another problem due to its fat content, caffeine and allergic reactions for many.

Fortunately there are alternatives. These recipes are favorites made with natural foods that are great tasting and so much better nutritionally. The best part is knowing that these desserts are health-building whole foods, and not simply empty calories.

Whole wheat pastry flour should be used when making desserts. Ground from soft wheat berries, pastry flour should be very finely ground to achieve the texture and moistness necessary for cakes and other similar desserts. Coarser, whole wheat flours simply will not produce the same results. As mentioned earlier, it is of great advantage to grind your own flour for optimum freshness, texture and flavor. If you choose to purchase flour, try Walnut Acres flours, which are superior in fine texture. One step which is necessary in preparing flour for desserts is sifting. Always remember to sift the dry ingredients together before adding. If you are using a coarse grade of flour, quite a bit of bran will be removed. Simply save the coarse bran for use when baking breads, cookies or crackers.

Carob powder will be substituted for chocolate in all recipes. Compared to chocolate, carob is low in fat, contains more fiber, is naturally sweet, and contains no caffeine. Carob has a different flavor than chocolate but many actually prefer the taste of carob, even former chocolate "addicts." If you find yourself longing for some chocolate brownies or cake or cookies, try one of these carob recipes and you will be more than satisfied. Carob chips can be purchased in natural food stores or in many supermarkets now. Some contain sugar, some do not, so purchase those without sugar, if available.

The recipes in this chapter range from quick and easy to absolutely elegant for very special occasions. Since these desserts are good for you, you can enjoy them whenever you like without feeling guilty. Now that's a treat!

APPLE PIE†

An American tradition.

Double recipe of Basic Pie Crust (see index)
  with 2 teaspoons cinnamon and ½ teaspoon
  nutmeg added to the flour mixture
7 cups sliced tart apples, unpeeled

⅔ cup honey
1 teaspoon cinnamon
¼ teaspoon nutmeg

Prepare a double recipe of the Basic Pie Crust, but add the 2 teaspoons cinnamon and ½ teaspoon nutmeg to the flour mixture before cutting in the butter. Divide the dough in half and roll out half for the bottom of the pie shell. Mix together the apples, honey, 1 teaspoon cinnamon and ¼ teaspoon nutmeg and then spoon into the pie shell. Roll out the remaining pie crust dough and place over the apple mixture. Perforate the top pie crust with a fork or knife in any pattern or design you like. Bake in a preheated oven at 400°F. for 50–60 minutes or until golden brown. It's a good idea to place a cookie sheet under your pie pan to catch drips. Serve with vanilla ice cream for pie à la mode!

Note: Do not peel the apples, as the peels become very soft and the fiber is good for you. Plus, if you use red apples they give the filling a rosy color.

† No Added Salt.

FRESH CHERRY PIE

A delicious summer dessert when fresh cherries are available.

Double recipe of Basic Pie Crust (see index)
4 cups sweet Bing cherries, pitted, sliced in
  half or whole
⅓ cup honey

⅓ cup whole wheat flour
dash salt
1 tablespoon butter

Prepare a double recipe of the Basic Pie Crust. Roll out half the dough and line a 9 inch pie plate. Roll out the other half, and cut into narrow strips to be used later in a lattice top.
Combine the cherries, honey, flour and salt together, mixing well. Pour the mixture into the prepared, unbaked pie crust. Dot with butter, then arrange the lattice pastry strips on top in a basket weave fashion. Flute edges. Bake in a preheated oven at 400°F. for 50–55 minutes. Makes one 9 inch pie.

Note: The recipe calls for sweet cherries, since fresh tart pie cherries are often difficult to locate. However, if you have access to the tart variety, and wish to use them instead, it will be necessary to increase the honey to ⅔ of a cup to successfully sweeten the pie.

PUMPKIN PIE

A delicious dessert for the traditional holiday dinners.

1 unbaked Basic Pie Crust (see index)
½ teaspoon cinnamon
1½ cups cooked pumpkin, pureed
⅓ cup honey
1 tablespoon molasses
3 eggs, beaten
¼ teaspoon salt

½ teaspoon ground ginger
1 cup water
1 cup nonfat dry milk powder
1 teaspoon cinnamon
⅛ teaspoon allspice
¼ teaspoon nutmeg

Prepare a Basic Pie Crust according to the directions, adding ½ teaspoon cinnamon to the flour mixture before the ice water is added. Combine the pumpkin, honey, molasses and eggs and mix until smooth. Stir in the spices, water and milk until well blended. Pour the pumpkin mixture into the prepared unbaked pie crust and bake in a preheated oven at 425°F. for 15 minutes. Then turn the heat down to 350°F. and continue to bake for 1 hour or until a knife inserted in the center comes out clean. Allow to cool completely, then cover and refrigerate. Serve topped with Whipped Cream, (see index).

COCONUT CREAM PIE

Creamy and delicious.

1 Coconut Pie Crust (see index)
⅓ cup whole wheat flour
¼ teaspoon salt
2 cups skim milk
1 cup dried unsweetened coconut

⅓ cup honey
2 egg yolks, beaten
1 teaspoon vanilla
1 tablespoon butter
Whipped Cream (see index)

Prepare the Coconut Pie Crust and bake, then cool. In the top of a double boiler, combine the flour and salt, then slowly add the milk, stirring continuously. Stir in the honey and coconut and cook until thick, 10–15 minutes. Continue to cook for another 10 minutes, stirring frequently. Add a spoonful of the milk mixture to the egg yolks, mixing well, then add this to the rest of the milk mixture and continue to cook and stir for another minute. Take the filling off the heat and stir in the vanilla and butter until well blended. Allow the filling to cool then pour into the prepared pie crust. Refrigerate. Top with the Whipped Cream and sprinkle with dried coconut flakes.

BANANA-COCONUT CREAM PIE

Follow the basic Coconut Cream Pie recipe, but just before spooning the cooled filling into the pie crust, slice 3 ripe bananas into the bottom of the pie crust, then pour the cooled filling on top. Top with whipped cream and garnish with dried coconut flakes.

COCONUT PUDDING

Follow the basic Coconut Cream Pie recipe, but omit the pie crust. When the filling is done cooking, spoon into four dessert bowls and allow to cool. Refrigerate if not eaten at once. Serve topped with Whipped Cream, (see index). Serves 4.

VARIATION: • Allow the filling mixture to cool and stir sliced bananas into the pudding before placing in the bowls.

Carob Dessert Crêpes with Carob Fudge Sauce

FRESH STRAWBERRY CHEESECAKE†

This is so good it's hard to believe it's high in protein too! Enjoy the sweet creaminess without feeling guilty.

CRUST:

1 cup wheat germ
1 cup finely chopped almonds
1 cup whole wheat flour
2 teaspoons cinnamon

¼ teaspoon allspice
½ teaspoon nutmeg
¼ cup soft butter
¼ cup honey

Mix together the wheat germ, almonds, flour and spices. Cut the butter into the mixture and then add the honey. Mix well and press into a springform or 9 inch square baking pan. Make sure the crust is a uniform thickness.

BATTER:

6 eggs
1 cup unflavored yogurt
2½ cups cream cheese
juice of one lemon
¾ cup honey

1 teaspoon vanilla
¼ teaspoon cinnamon
⅛ teaspoon allspice
⅛ teaspoon nutmeg

Mix all the ingredients in a food processor or blender until smooth and creamy. Gently pour into the prepared crust and bake in a preheated oven at 300°F. for 2 hours or until golden, puffed in appearance and slightly dry to the touch. Cool on a rack 10 minutes, (it will fall slightly) and then refrigerate 6–8 hours before serving. Meanwhile clean a pint of fresh strawberries and remove the stems. Just before serving, top the cheesecake with the strawberries and enjoy the comps.

† No Added Salt.

DOUBLE CAROB CHEESECAKE†

Very rich and creamy.

CRUST:

¾ cup whole wheat flour
½ cup carob powder
1 cup ground almonds

½ cup wheat germ
¼ cup softened butter
¼ cup honey

Combine the dry ingredients until well mixed, then cut in the butter and blend in the honey. This is easiest in a food processor but you can do it with your hands too. Press this mixture into a springform cheesecake pan or 9 inch square baking pan.

FILLING:

16 ounces cream cheese
6 eggs
¾ cup honey
¼ cup smooth peanut butter

⅔ cup nonfat dry milk
⅓ cup sifted carob powder
½ cup cold water

Combine all ingredients in a blender or food processor and blend until smooth, scraping sides frequently. Gently pour into the pressed crust mixture and bake in a preheated oven at 300°F. for 2–2½ hours or until high and puffed uniformly. Cool briefly at room temperature then refrigerate and chill for several hours before eating. Once the cheesecake has chilled, cover with foil to retain freshness. Serves 12.

† No Added Salt.

APPLE NUT CAKE

This cake makes its own topping, and is great as a coffee cake as well as a dessert cake.

2 cups whole wheat flour, sifted
1 teaspoon baking soda
½ teaspoon salt
¼ cup soft butter
2 eggs, beaten
3 tablespoons honey

1 cup unflavored yogurt
¼ cup unsweetened coconut
¼ cup chopped almonds, pecans or walnuts
2½ cups sliced apples
1 teaspoon cinnamon
2 tablespoons honey

Sift the flour, soda and salt, then cut in the butter, using a food processor or pastry blender. Beat the eggs, yogurt and 3 tablespoons of honey together then stir into the flour mixture. The dough will be very stiff, but don't worry, it tastes moist when it's done! Lightly butter the sides of a 9 inch square springform pan. Then sprinkle the coconut on the bottom, followed by a layer of nuts, then apples, then cinnamon and finally drizzle the 2 tablespoons of honey over the apples. Now carefully spread the dough over the layers, trying to disturb them as little as possible. Bake in a preheated oven at 350°F. for 40–45 minutes, or until the cake tests done with a toothpick. As soon as it's out of the oven, loosen sides with a knife and turn out on a large plate or cake pan. Serve warm with vanilla ice cream if you like. Serves 6.

BANANA CAROB CHIP CAKE†

Very moist and sweet.

1 cup banana puree (or about 2 large bananas
  pureed in the blender)
½ cup soft butter
4 egg yolks, beaten
⅓ cup unflavored yogurt
⅔ cup honey

2⅓ cups whole wheat flour
1 tablespoon baking powder
½ cup carob chips
4 egg whites, beaten stiff
1½ teaspoon vanilla

Combine the banana, butter, egg yolks, yogurt and honey in a large bowl, and beat until smooth. Sift together the flour and baking powder and slowly add to the banana mixture, stirring continuously. When well blended, stir in the carob chips, then fold in the egg whites and vanilla. Pour into an oiled and floured 9 × 13 inch baking pan or two 8 inch round cake pans. Bake in a preheated oven at 350°F. for 30–35 minutes. Test with a toothpick and be sure not to over-bake and dry out the cake. When cool, frost with Carob Peanut Butter Frosting (see index).

VARIATION: • This will also make about 20 cupcakes. Reduce baking time to 20 minutes and use paper liners in your muffin pans.

† No Added Salt.

CAROB CAKE†

A delicious moist birthday treat!

½ cup soft butter
⅔ cup honey
4 egg yolks, beaten
2 cups sifted whole wheat flour (This removes some bran; save it for other baking.)

⅔ cup carob powder
1 tablespoon baking powder
¾ cup unflavored yogurt
4 egg whites, beaten stiff
1½ teaspoons vanilla

Cream butter and honey together. Stir beaten egg yolks into the mixture. Sift dry ingredients together and add to egg mixture alternately with the yogurt. Fold in the beaten egg whites and add vanilla. Turn into an oiled and flour-dusted 9 × 13 inch baking pan or two 8 inch round cake pans. Bake 30–40 minutes in a preheated oven at 350°F. Test with a toothpick and be sure not to overbake and dry out the cake. When cool, frost with Carob Peanut Butter Frosting (see index).

† No Added Salt.

CAROB PEANUT BUTTER FROSTING†

3 tablespoons soft butter
3 tablespoons peanut butter
2 tablespoons honey

¼ cup warm water
½ cup milk powder
⅓ cup carob powder, sifted

Combine the butter, peanut butter, honey and water. Then stir in milk powder and carob and beat well. Frost cooled cake then sprinkle with chopped peanuts, coconut or other nuts.

† No Added Salt.

CARROT CAKE

A light, moist delicious cake.

6 egg yolks, beaten
⅔ cup honey
1½ cups grated carrots
½ teaspoon vanilla
1 cup sifted whole wheat flour

½ teaspoon salt
1 teaspoon cinnamon
½ teaspoon nutmeg
6 egg whites, beaten stiff

Mix together the egg yolks, honey, grated carrots and vanilla. Sift together the flour, salt, nutmeg and cinnamon. Alternately fold the egg yolk mixture and flour into the stiff egg whites. Keep the stirring to a minimum. Gently turn into a lightly buttered and floured 9 × 9 inch square pan or a tube pan. Bake in a preheated oven at 325°F. for 1 hour and 15 minutes or until golden and the cake springs back when touched. Invert to cool in pan. Frost with Cream Cheese Frosting (see index).

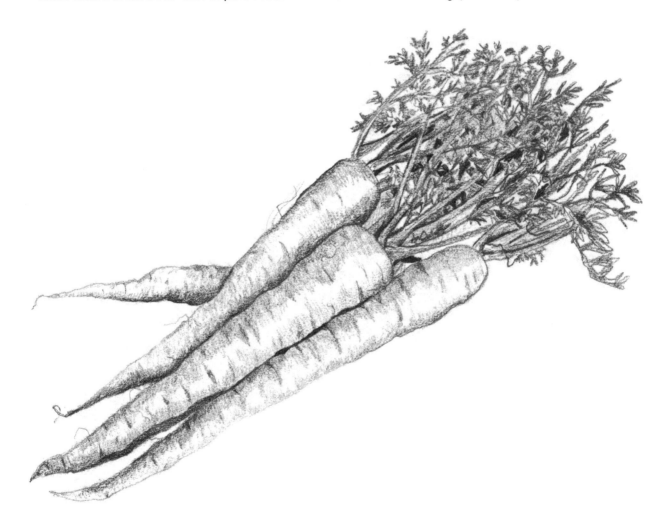

CREAM CHEESE FROSTING†

8 ounces cream cheese, softened
1 cup butter, softened

⅓ cup honey
1 teaspoon vanilla

Cream the cream cheese and butter together until well blended. Beat in the honey and then the vanilla. Keep the frosting refrigerated, as well as the cake once it is frosted.

† No Added Salt.

CHRISTMAS FRUITCAKE†

If you love dried fruit and nuts, you'll love this!

½ cup honey
⅓ cup apple juice
¼ cup molasses
5 egg yolks, beaten
6 tablespoons soft butter
2 tablespoons oil
2 cups raisins
¾ cup chopped dates
½ cup diced dried pineapple

¼ cup chopped dried apricots
1⅓ cup whole wheat flour
1 cup chopped almonds
1 cup chopped walnuts
1 teaspoon cinnamon
1 teaspoon allspice
¼ teaspoon nutmeg
⅛ teaspoon ginger
5 egg whites, beaten stiff

Mix the honey, apple juice, molasses, egg yolks, butter and oil together in a large bowl. Combine the dried fruit, flour, nuts and spices in a separate bowl, mixing well. Add the fruit mixture to the honey mixture, stirring well, then fold in the stiffly beaten egg whites. Place in two loaf pans you have prepared by oiling first, then lining with wax paper. Bake in a preheated oven at 275°F. for about 2 hours or until cakes test done. Place a shallow pan filled with water in the oven while baking. When the cakes are nearly finished baking and the tops are still moist, you may decorate the tops with almonds, pecans or dried fruit arranged in any pattern you like. Then finish baking. When the fruitcakes are cool, store in the refrigerator, tightly wrapped in foil. Flavor improves as they "age." Makes 2 fruitcakes.

† No Added Salt.

CAROB DESSERT CRÊPES

So elegant, and delicious too!

Follow the basic Crêpe recipe (see index), with the following additions. In a small bowl, mix together 6 tablespoons carob powder, ¼ cup very hot water, and 2 tablespoons honey. Stir until well blended and allow to cool. When mixing the crêpe batter in the basic crêpe recipe, add this carob mixture to it, blend and allow to rest 2 hours or longer. Cook as in the basic recipe. When cool, separate the crêpes with sheets of wax paper and wrap in aluminum foil, keeping them flat. Store the crêpes in the refrigerator or freezer until 1–2 hours before serving, then remove and allow to warm to room temperature.

To make the filling, combine: **2 cups whipping cream**
2½ tablespoons honey
2 teaspoons vanilla extract

Beat the cream mixture in a large bowl until it forms stiff peaks. Spoon 2–3 tablespoons of the whipped cream along the center of each crepe and roll into a cylindrical tube shape. Arrange on a serving platter side-by-side and top with Carob Fudge Sauce (see index) and sprinkle with ¼ cup chopped walnuts or slivered almonds. Makes 14, 8 inch crêpes or 7 servings.

CAROB FUDGE SAUCE†

Delicious on ice cream, crêpes, bananas or whatever you like.

⅓ cup carob powder, sifted
⅓ cup nonfat dry milk powder
2 tablespoons honey

1 tablespoon smooth peanut butter
½ cup hot water

Combine the carob and the dry milk in a small saucepan, mixing well. Then stir in the honey, peanut butter and hot water. Beat until smooth and well blended over low heat. This should take about five minutes. Serve hot or cold. This sauce can be stored in the refrigerator for about one week. Makes about ½ cup sauce.

† No Added Salt.

APPLE CRISP

A wonderful use for extra autumn apples.

1¼ cups whole wheat flour
¼ cup wheat germ
1 cup rolled oat flakes
½ teaspoon baking soda
¼ teaspoon salt
½ cup soft butter

¼ cup molasses
½ cup honey
5 cups sliced apples
1 tablespoon cinnamon
2 tablespoons honey
2 teaspoons lemon juice

Mix together the flour, wheat germ, oats, baking soda and salt. Cut the butter into the mixture and then mix in the molasses and the ½ cup of honey. In a separate bowl, mix the apples, cinnamon, 2 tablespoons honey and lemon juice. Turn the apple mixture into a 9 inch square buttered baking dish and then cover with the flour mixture. Bake in a preheated oven at 350°F. for 45 minutes or until golden brown. Extra tasty warm with natural Vanilla Ice Cream, (see index).

CAROB BROWNIES†

Many recipes were experimented with to finally arrive at this extra moist and fudge-like dessert.

⅓ cup soft butter
⅔ cup honey
4 eggs, beaten well
¼ cup unflavored yogurt
⅓ cup creamy peanut butter

1 teaspoon vanilla
½ cup milk powder
¾ cup carob powder
¾ cup whole wheat flour

Cream together the butter, honey, eggs, yogurt, peanut butter and vanilla. Stir in the milk powder, carob and flour. Pour into a buttered 9 inch square baking pan and bake in a preheated oven at 325°F. for 30–35 minutes or until a toothpick inserted comes out clean. Allow to cool slightly then cut into squares. Or before cutting, frost with Carob Peanut Butter Frosting (see index). Makes 16 brownies.

VARIATION: • Add 1 cup chopped peanuts, walnuts *or* almonds before baking.

Note: These brownies are tastiest if kept in the freezer, and eaten while still cold. They don't seem to get hard; just cut them into squares and place in a freezer bag.

† No Added Salt.

VANILLA ICE CREAM

A recipe using honey for your ice cream freezer.

1 quart half and half
2 eggs, beaten
½ cup honey

1 tablespoon vanilla
⅛ teaspoon salt

Combine all the ingredients, mixing well. Chill in the refrigerator then process according to your ice cream freezer's instructions. Makes about 1½ quarts.

CAROB CHIP ICE CREAM

Add 1 cup carob chips to the Vanilla Ice Cream after it has frozen to the soft, mushy stage. Then continue freezing until done. Makes about 1½ quarts.

STRAWBERRY ICE CREAM

Add 2 cups sliced strawberries sweetened with ¼ cup honey to the basic Vanilla Ice Cream recipe. Makes about 2 quarts.

VARIATION: • Substitute peaches, raspberries, cherries or pineapple for the strawberries.

WHIPPED CREAM†

An elegant dessert topping.

½ cup heavy cream
½ teaspoon vanilla

2 teaspoons honey

Combine the cream, vanilla and honey and beat until doubled in volume and peaks are formed. Keep refrigerated or serve at once. This will be enough for an entire pie, gingerbread or most any other dessert. This can be frozen for later use by placing it in an airtight container once it has been whipped. To use, simply scoop out what you need and allow a few minutes to defrost. Makes about 1 cup.

† Salt Free.

SUPER FUDGE†

Delicious, chewy, sweet and full of protein.

1 cup smooth peanut butter
1 cup honey
1 cup carob powder
1 cup raisins
1 cup unsweetened dried coconut

⅓ cup walnuts, chopped
½ cup raw sunflower seeds
⅔ cup raw sesame seeds

In a small sauce pan combine the peanut butter and honey, and cook over medium low heat to just before boiling. Stir in the carob until well blended then add the rest of the ingredients. Turn into a buttered 8 × 8 inch pan and place in the refrigerator to harden. When cool, cut into 1 inch squares. Keep refrigerated. Makes 36 small pieces.

† No Added Salt.

CARAMELS†

A rich treat to enjoy at Christmas, or for any special occasion.

½ cup butter, soft
1¼ cups honey
2 tablespoons molasses

2 cups half and half
½ teaspoon vanilla
½ cup chopped nuts (optional)

Mix butter, honey, molasses and 1 cup half and half in a saucepan and cook slowly over low heat until mixture thickens and forms a soft ball when dropped in a cup of cold water. Add the remaining half and half and continue cooking until caramel reaches the firm ball stage. This process takes 1½–2 hours and requires constant stirring, so get a chair for yourself and a book you've been meaning to read. When the caramel reaches the firm ball stage, remove from the heat and stir in the vanilla and nuts if you are using them. Pour into a buttered 8 inch square pan and allow to cool. Cut into ¾ inch squares and wrap individually in wax paper.

† No Added Salt.

HALVAH†

A Turkish candy that is actually good for you!

½ cup almonds
⅓ cup wheat germ
½ cup unsweetened dried coconut

¼ cup tahini (sesame butter)
¼ cup honey

In a blender or food processor, finely grind the almonds, wheat germ and coconut. Then add the tahini and honey and continue processing until the mixture begins to form a ball. Knead by hand briefly then divide in half. Shape each half into a rectangular shape about an inch thick, or roll into a 1 inch thick coil. Wrap in wax paper and refrigerate until firm. Cut off small slices when ready to serve.

† No Added Salt.

CAROB HALVAH†

Follow the basic Halvah recipe, with one exception. Before kneading the mixture, add ¼ cup of carob powder to the dough and fold in. This produces a marbling effect. Make sure all the carob powder becomes moistened with the halvah mixture. Then shape and refrigerate as before.

† No Added Salt.

CAROB TREAT†

A simple, quick instant "candy."

2 tablespoons carob powder   **1 tablespoon peanut butter**
4 tablespoons instant nonfat milk   **2 tablespoons hot water**

Mix the carob powder and milk together in a cup. Then stir in the peanut butter and water. This will be a very thick, fudge-like treat to be savored slowly with a spoon. You can turn it into a carob sauce topping for ice cream by adding slightly more water. Some prefer a touch of honey, but since carob powder is naturally sweet it's really not necessary. This is high in protein too! Makes 1 serving.

VARIATION: • Add a tablespoon of coconut, peanuts or other nuts.

† No Added Salt.

FROZEN BANANAS†

A popular summertime treat.

Peel bananas and dip into orange juice to prevent discoloring. Press a wooden stick into the length of each banana, and freeze on a cookie sheet until solid. Eat as is, or spoon Carob Fudge Sauce (see index) onto the frozen bananas and sprinkle with chopped nuts. Eat immediately or re-freeze. Once well frozen, the bananas should be covered with plastic wrap to keep them fresh.

† No Added Salt.

POPSICLES†

An easy summer-time cooler.

**natural pure fruit juices such as pear, grape,
apple, orange or pineapple**

First of all you must purchase an inexpensive plastic popsicle mold. Most make eight popsicles. Now pour in your favorite chilled fruit juice. Pear and pineapple juices are very sweet and make excellent popsicles. Another option is to fill the molds halfway with one flavor, freeze then pour in another flavor, insert tops and freeze again. Or mix flavors together. The choice is up to you and it couldn't be easier. To remove from the molds, simply run warm water over the plastic. Makes 8 popsicles.

† Salt Free.

YOGURT BARS†

A low calorie ice cream substitute for the whole family.

1½ cups unflavored yogurt
**¾ cup fresh or frozen fruit, unsweetened
  (strawberry, banana or pineapple)**

2 tablespoons honey

Place the yogurt and fruit in the blender, but do not blend. Place in the freezer for 1 to 2 hours, or until the mixture is just beginning to freeze. Now add the honey and blend until well mixed and the fruit is pureed. Spoon into a popsicle mold and freeze until solid. Release from the mold by running warm water over the mold. Makes 8 frozen treats.

† Salt Free.

YOGURT DREAM BARS†

This is a favorite way to make frozen treats.

2 cups unflavored yogurt
1½ tablespoons honey

5½ tablespoons frozen orange juice
concentrate, unsweetened

Place the yogurt and honey in the blender, but do not blend. Place in the freezer about 2 hours, or until the yogurt is just beginning to freeze. Now add the frozen orange juice concentrate and blend until smooth. Spoon into a popsicle mold, (most make 8 individual popsicles), and freeze until solid. Release from mold by running warm water over the plastic. Makes 8 frozen treats.

† Salt Free.

PINA COLADA YOGURT BARS†

A nice dessert bar.

1½ cups unflavored yogurt
¾ cup unsweetened fresh or canned pineapple

3 tablespoons, unsweetened dried coconut
2 tablespoons honey

Place all the ingredients in the blender and blend until smooth. Now place the blender in the freezer and allow to become partially frozen. This takes several hours. Now stir or blend for just a moment to re-mix, then spoon into a popsicle mold. Freeze until firm. Remove from the mold by running warm water over the outside of the mold.

† Salt Free.

CHAPTER TEN

Cookies

From left to right: Coconut Macaroons, Carob Pinwheels, Fig Bars, Carob Chip Cookies and Christmas Cookies

CHAPTER TEN

Cookies

Cookies are an ideal snack or dessert for many reasons. A well-known favorite of children and adults alike, they are a take-anywhere food that stores well, and if made with wholesome ingredients they are good for you too!

The recipes included here vary from rolled and drop cookies and bars to one made without baking. Some are so full of nuts, dried fruit, molasses, yogurt and other vitamin- and protein-rich ingredients that they are nutritious enough to substitute as a breakfast for reluctant or hurried eaters.

When making these cookies, chill the dough before baking to make it easier to handle, since cookie dough made with honey tends to be a bit sticky. You can make several batches at once and refrigerate or freeze the dough until ready to use for "instant" home-baked hot cookies.

Finely ground pastry flour is necessary for cookie dough that is rolled and for the more delicate cookies, but a coarser ground flour is suitable for the rest.

When baking cookies, always remember to preheat your oven, and place the baking sheets close to the center of the oven to prevent cookies from over-browning on the top or burning on the bottom. Centering the sheets in the oven also aids in proper circulation and helps ensure that all the cookies will be evenly done.

Cool the cookies completely on wire racks and then store in airtight containers. If you are making more than one variety of cookie, each kind should be stored separately to prevent the flavors from mixing. If the cookies will be around longer than a week (a rare occurrence), refrigerate or freeze them to keep them fresh.

OATMEAL RAISIN COOKIES

Popular with young and old.

1½ cups whole wheat flour
3 cups rolled oat flakes
½ teaspoon salt
1 teaspoon baking soda
1 teaspoon cinnamon
½ teaspoon nutmeg

¾ cup raisins
½ cup soft butter
2 eggs, beaten
⅓ cup unflavored yogurt
¾ cup honey

Mix the flour, oat flakes, salt, soda and spices together. Then add raisins and separate them in the flour mixture. In a large bowl combine the butter, eggs, yogurt and honey. Blend well then add the flour mixture and stir. Drop on lightly oiled cookie sheets with a tablespoon, leaving room for the cookies to spread. Bake in a preheated oven at 325°F. for 10 minutes or until golden brown. Makes 3–4 dozen cookies.

VARIATION: • Add ½ cup chopped walnuts.

PEANUT BUTTER COOKIES

1 cup peanut butter
¼ cup soft butter
½ cup honey
¼ cup molasses
1 egg, beaten

½ teaspoon vanilla
2 cups whole wheat flour
½ teaspoon baking soda
¼ teaspoon salt
½ cup chopped roasted, unsalted peanuts

In a large bowl combine all ingredients in first column and beat until well blended. Add the flour, soda and salt and mix well. Fold in the nuts then chill the dough for 2 hours or more. Drop the dough by the tablespoonful on lightly oiled baking sheets. Press down the tops with a fork in a criss-cross manner. Bake in a preheated oven at 325°F. for 10–15 minutes or until golden brown. Makes 3 dozen cookies.

VARIATION: • Add ½ cup carob chips when the peanuts are folded in.

CAROB CHIP COOKIES

Always a favorite.

2¼ cups whole wheat flour
1 teaspoon baking soda
½ teaspoon salt
½ cup soft butter
⅔ cup honey

2 tablespoons molasses
2 eggs, beaten
1 teaspoon vanilla
2 cups carob chips

Stir together the flour, soda and salt. In a large bowl, cream together the butter, honey and molasses. Beat in the egg, then the vanilla. Stir in the flour mixture, then the carob chips. Drop by teaspoonfuls on to lightly oiled cookie sheets and bake in a preheated oven at 375°F. for 10–12 minutes. Makes 4–5 dozen cookies.

VARIATIONS: • DOUBLE CAROB: subtract ¼ cup flour and add ¼ cup carob.
• PEANUT BUTTER CAROB: subtract ¼ cup butter and add ¼ cup peanut butter and ½ cup chopped peanuts.
• DOUBLE CAROB PEANUT BUTTER: combine *both* variations!

CHRISTMAS COOKIES

Just like the "sugar" cookies you remember.

2 cups whole wheat flour
1 teaspoon baking powder
¼ teaspoon salt
½ teaspoon cinnamon
½ cup soft butter

½ cup honey
1 egg, beaten
1 teaspoon vanilla
1½ tablespoons lemon juice

Stir together the dry ingredients. Cream together the butter and honey in a large bowl. Beat in the egg, then vanilla and lemon juice. Add the flour mixture and stir well.

Divide dough in half, wrap each in an airtight container or plastic wrap and chill for several hours. Roll out ⅛ inch thick and cut with cookie cutters. Place on lightly oiled cookie sheets. To decorate, sprinkle with unsweetened dried shredded coconut, tinted with Natural Food Coloring (see index) if you desire, or place carob chips, nuts, raisins or other dried fruit on cookie shapes before baking. Bake in a preheated oven at 350°F. for 8–10 minutes. Makes 4–5 dozen cookies.

NATURAL FOOD COLORING†

Red: boil a beet until tender, mash, sieve and use the juice.
Green: boil spinach until tender, mash, sieve and use the juice.
Yellow: boil a carrot until tender, mash, sieve and use the juice.
Purple: cook blueberries until tender, mash, sieve and use the juice.
Pink: cook strawberries until tender, mash, sieve and use the juice.
Brown: add a small amount of carob powder and a few drops of water.

† Salt Free.

CAROB PINWHEELS

Follow the basic Christmas Cookies recipe with the following changes. After the dough is mixed, divide it in half and work in 2 tablespoons carob powder to one half of the mixture. Chill both halves in the refrigerator for several hours. Then roll out each piece of dough separately to a rectangle, 8 inches wide, about 16 inches long and ⅛ inch thick. Place the carob dough on top of the plain dough, fitting together as well as possible. Roll together lightly, then beginning with the 16 inch side roll the layers of dough together, jelly roll fashion. Press the edges down on the roll, then wrap in wax paper and chill for another hour. When chilled, slice through the roll at ⅛ to ¼ inch intervals and place the cookies on lightly oiled baking sheets. Bake in a preheated oven at 350°F. for 10–15 minutes, depending on thickness, or until golden brown. Makes about 4 dozen cookies.

COCONUT MACAROONS†

Easy to make and sure to please.

3¼ cups unsweetened dried coconut
½ cup whole wheat flour
4 eggs, beaten
⅔ cup honey

2 teaspoons vanilla
⅓ cup chopped walnuts *or* almonds
½ cup chopped dates

Mix together the coconut and flour. Then stir in the eggs, honey and vanilla. Add the walnuts and dates and mix well. To shape the cookies, scoop the mixture into a ¼ cup oiled measuring cup or ice cream scoop and place on a lightly oiled cookie sheet. These will not rise or alter in shape while baking, so form nice little mounds. Bake in a preheated oven at 325°F. for 30–35 minutes or until golden brown. Makes 16 macaroons.

VARIATION: • Add ½ cup carob powder to the coconut and flour and omit the dates. So delicious!

† Salt Free.

GINGERBREAD COOKIES

Soft and puffy like cake. Makes great gingerbread men!

¾ **cup butter, soft**	**1 teaspoon baking soda**
¾ **cup molasses**	**4½ cups whole wheat flour**
¾ **cup honey**	**1 tablespoon ginger**
2 eggs, beaten	**1 teaspoon cinnamon**
1 cup buttermilk	**¼ teaspoon salt**

Cream together the butter, molasses, honey and eggs. Dissolve the baking soda in the buttermilk and add to the butter mixture. In a separate bowl combine the flour and spices, add to the butter mixture and stir well. Chill in the refrigerator 2 hours or longer. Remove about half the dough, and roll out as quickly as possible to prevent warming. This dough is very sticky and must be worked with quickly or you will have to add more flour to keep it from sticking to the table. Using as little flour as possible, roll to about ¼ inch thick and cut into desired shapes. Place on lightly oiled baking sheets. Adorn your gingerbread men, women and other shapes with raisins and nuts. Bake in a preheated oven at 375°F. for about 12 minutes. These are delicious as they are, or you can spread them with cream cheese or Cream Cheese Frosting (see index). Makes 3–4 dozen cookies.

THREE-IN-ONE COOKIE

Can't decide which cookie to make? Try this delicious combination of Oatmeal, Coconut and Carob Chip Cookies.

2 cups unsweetened dried coconut	¾ **cup honey**
1 cup whole wheat flour	**2 tablespoons molasses**
1 cup rolled oat flakes	**2 eggs, beaten**
1 teaspoon baking soda	**1 teaspoon vanilla**
½ **teaspoon salt**	**1½ cups carob chips**
½ **cup soft butter**	

Combine the dry ingredients. In a large bowl, cream the butter, honey, molasses and eggs together, then stir in the vanilla. Add the coconut mixture, blending well, then mix in the carob chips. Drop by teaspoonfuls on lightly oiled cookie sheets and bake in a preheated oven at 350°F. for 10 minutes, or until golden brown. Cool on wire racks and store in a tightly closed container. Makes 6 dozen cookies.

FIG BARS

Sweet and chewy.

2 cups chopped dried figs
¾ cup water
⅓ cup honey
4 tablespoons lemon juice
½ cup unsweetened dried coconut
1½ cups whole wheat flour

1½ cups rolled oat flakes
½ teaspoon salt
¼ cup soft butter
¼ cup honey
1 teaspoon vanilla

Put figs, water, ⅓ cup honey, 3 tablespoons of the lemon juice and ¼ cup of the coconut in a small sauce pan and cook on low heat until thick. Meanwhile mix together the flour, oat flakes, ¼ cup coconut and salt. Then cut in the butter, and add the ¼ cup honey, vanilla and 1 tablespoon lemon juice, mixing well. Press half the flour mixture into a buttered 9 inch square baking pan. Cover with the fig mixture, then put the rest of the flour mixture on top. Bake in a preheated oven at 350°F. for 35 minutes or until golden brown. Allow to cool and cut into squares. Makes 16 square bars.

VARIATION: • Use dates instead of figs: Date Bars!

SCOTCH SHORTBREAD†

½ cup soft butter
¼ cup honey
1 egg

½ teaspoon vanilla
1½ cups whole wheat flour

Mix together the butter, honey, egg and vanilla. Stir in the flour until well blended and refrigerate 2 hours or more. In an oiled and floured 9 inch square pan, press the dough out evenly and cut into small squares. Prick each square with a fork and bake in a preheated oven at 350°F. for about 15 minutes, or until golden brown. Makes 4 dozen small cookies.

VARIATION: • Add 1 cup dried unsweetened coconut flakes and ¼ cup maple syrup to the recipe.

† No Added Salt.

"EAGLE" BARS†

No mixing makes these rich bars as easy as they are good.

¼ pound butter
**1 cup graham cracker crumbs [make your own
  (see index), or buy those made from whole
  wheat sold in natural food stores]**
1½ cups carob chips

1 cup unsweetened dried coconut
1 cup finely chopped almonds *or* walnuts
⅓ cup honey
1 cup nonfat dry milk
water

Melt the butter in a 9 × 13 inch baking dish. Sprinkle a layer of cracker crumbs, then a layer of carob chips, a layer of coconut and finally a layer of nuts. Measure the honey in a small bowl, then add water to the measuring cup filled with the dry milk until you have one cup of thick liquid milk. Add the milk to the honey, stir well, and drizzle over the layers of nuts, chips and crumbs. Bake in a preheated oven at 325°F. for 30–40 minutes, or until golden on top. Cut into bars when cool.

† No Added Salt.

STRAWBERRY APPLE BARS†

Sweet and chewy.

1 cup unsweetened dried coconut
1 cup flaked oats
1 cup whole wheat flour
¼ cup soft butter
¼ cup honey

½ teaspoon vanilla
1 tablespoon lemon juice
1¼ cups apple slices
½ cup strawberry preserves made with honey
½ teaspoon cinnamon

Combine the coconut, oats and flour. Cut in the butter, then stir in the honey, vanilla and lemon juice, mixing well. Press half the mixture in a buttered 9 inch square pan, reserving the rest. Heat the apple slices, preserves and cinnamon together over low heat in a small saucepan, stirring frequently until thick and bubbly. Spoon the fruit mixture over the pressed coconut mixture, until evenly distributed. Sprinkle the remaining coconut mixture over the top of the fruit and bake in a preheated oven at 350°F. for 30–35 minutes or until golden brown. Allow to cool and cut into bars. Makes 16 bars.

VARIATION: • Substitute peach or raspberry preserves made with honey for the strawberry. You can make your own, or buy them at natural food stores.

† No added salt.

PEANUT BUTTER BALLS†

⅔ cup peanut butter
⅓ cup carob powder
⅓ cup honey

⅓ cup sesame seeds
⅓ cup peanuts
unsweetened dried coconut flakes

Combine all ingredients except coconut and roll into bite-sized balls. Roll in coconut and keep refrigerated in a tightly closed container. Makes 2 dozen small confections.

† No Added Salt.

CHAPTER ELEVEN

Beverages

CHAPTER ELEVEN

Beverages

Beverages are a basic part of every meal and are delicious by themselves as well. There is an incredible variety of natural herb teas that do not contain caffeine, and some varieties are dark and robust enough to provide an excellent coffee substitute. Roastaroma® by Celestial Seasonings contains malt, barley, carob, chicory and other ingredients and brews a delicious coffee-like beverage. There are so many different types of herb teas, you're certain to find several you enjoy.

Fruit juices are an ideal natural beverage. Look for 100% pure fruit juice with no sugar or other ingredients added. Many fruit juices can be purchased "unfiltered" which means they were not refined with the resulting loss of pulp, vitamins and minerals. Unfiltered juices have a stronger fruit taste, but tend to be cloudy, with the pulp settling on the bottom. Always shake the bottle of unfiltered juice before serving to remix the particles.

Other ingredients for natural beverages include milk, yogurt, fruits, vegetables and nuts. Use skim milk wherever milk is called for or mix up nonfat dry milk powder. If you drink whole milk now, you can gradually switch to lowfat milk, by mixing the two, and then later go on to skim. It's a great way to decrease calories and lower your fat intake. (It's all a matter of what you are accustomed to.)

The beverages with yogurt are a great substitute for the packaged breakfast drinks, and you can also add ground nuts or nut butters to yogurt or milk drinks to add taste and increase the amount of protein. One of the best additives if you are looking for a drink that will substitute for a meal is nutritional brewer's yeast which is high in protein and loaded with B vitamins. Start with a ½ teaspoon at first as its taste is rather unusual if you are not used to it, and work up to 1–2 tablespoons of yeast per glass. This isn't the baking yeast but a food that many use as a supplement. You can also add molasses for iron and wheat germ for more protein and vitamins, but the mixture is bound to taste "healthy," which it certainly is, and not like a commercially made milk shake. Still, it's so good for you, especially if you are run down or under a lot of stress, you ought to give it a try.

Roastaroma® is a registered trademark of Celestial Seasonings, Inc.

HERBAL TEA†

There is a wide variety of herbal teas, from the mild camomile, peppermint, lemon grass and rosemary to rosehips (very high in vitamin C) and combination teas like Roastaroma.® Some are said to have therapeutic powers. Most varieties contain no caffeine or artificial ingredients. If you tried an herb tea once and didn't like it, don't despair. There are so many different kinds, you are sure to find others you do enjoy. You can purchase tea in either bags or loose pack, or you can grow it and dry it yourself. If you are using loose tea you will need a stainless steel tea ball or bamboo tea strainer. The metal tea ball tends to change the flavor of the tea, so the preferred way is to use a bamboo strainer. Or you can buy it in bag form which is more costly.

To brew the tea, heat 1 cup of water to boiling. Place one tea bag, or a tea ball with teaspoon of tea, in a cup and pour the hot water over it. Let steep, covered if possible, for 5 minutes. You can leave it longer if you prefer a very strong tea. Remove the tea from the cup and enjoy. Serves 1. Makes 8 ounces.

† Salt Free.

ICED TEA†

Follow the basic directions in Herbal Tea but allow 2 tea bags or 2 teaspoons tea for every cup hot water. Let steep for 5 minutes then remove the tea bags and pour over ice, adding more as necessary until very cold. Serve with lemon or lime wedges and honey if desired. Serves 1.

† Salt Free.

SUN TEA†

An easy way to save energy and have a lovely tea as well.

Fill a 2 quart glass jar with cold water and 8 tea bags (as described under Herbal Tea). The glass jar must be clear, and not heavily textured, to let the sun's rays in. Place the tea mixture in direct sunlight and leave for several hours until the tea has brewed to a nice rich color. Be sure the jar remains in the sun. It will take only 2 hours on a hot sunny day, but will require a longer time on cooler or partly sunny days. Serve it over ice or refrigerate for later use. Add lemon or lime wedges and honey to taste. Serves 8.

† Salt Free.

HOT RUSSIAN TEA†

So nice on a cold day, and soothing for a sore throat.

1 herb tea bag [Roastaroma® (by Celestial Seasonings) or Rosehips are good]
2 tablespoons frozen orange juice concentrate

2 tablespoons honey
1 tablespoon lemon juice
cinnamon

Brew the tea in one cup of boiling water for 5–7 minutes. Then add the orange juice concentrate, honey, lemon and stir well. Sprinkle cinnamon on top and drink at once. Serves 1.

† Salt Free.

MULLED CIDER†

Another great chill-chaser.

1 cup apple cider or juice
5 medium fresh or frozen strawberries

1, 2 inch piece cinnamon stick

Heat cider, strawberries and cinnamon to a boil, then simmer 10 minutes. Strain and serve. Serves 1.

† Salt Free.

APPLE BANANA DRINK†

Very sweet and good, especially appealing to babies and children.

⅔ cup sliced fresh banana   2 teaspoons lemon juice
1 cup unsweetened apple juice

Combine all ingredients in a blender and blend until smooth. Serve chilled. Makes 12 ounces.

† Salt Free.

CITRUS COOLER†

This is an excellent drink with hot popcorn.

¾ cup unsweetened orange juice   ¼ cup unsweetened grapefruit juice
½ cup unsweetened pineapple juice

Combine all ingredients in a tall glass over crushed ice. Makes 12 ounces.

† Salt Free.

MELON JUICE†

Place cubed watermelon, cantaloupe or honeydew in the blender and liquify. Serve cold over ice.

† Salt Free.

TROPICAL DELIGHT†

An exotic refresher.

¼ cup papaya concentrate   ½ cup pineapple juice
½ cup chilled water   ½ of a banana

Combine all the ingredients in a blender and liquify. Serve chilled. Makes 12 ounces.

† Salt Free.

Clockwise from top: Citrus Cooler, Strawberry Banana Milk Shake, Melon Juice, Hot Carob and Banapple Yogurt Milk Shake

TOMATO JUICE

Tomato juice can be made at the same time as Tomato Sauce. Please refer to the Tomato Sauce recipe (see index) and then do the following. In that portion of the recipe in which tomato juice has been saved in a bowl, take the juice and pour it through a sieve to catch all the remaining seeds. Add ¼ teaspoon salt for every pint of juice and stir well. Place in a covered non-metalic container and store in the refrigerator or freezer. Serve hot or cold.

VARIATION: • For salt free tomato juice, omit salt.

BANAPPLE YOGURT MILK SHAKE†

Thick and smooth, this is good at breakfast or as a treat.

⅔ cup sliced fresh bananas
⅔ cup unsweetened apple juice

⅔ cup yogurt, unflavored
cinnamon

Combine the apple juice and bananas in a blender and blend until smooth. Then stir in the yogurt and pour into two glasses. Sprinkle a dash of cinnamon on top. Serve chilled. Makes 14 ounces.

† Salt Free.

STRAWBERRY BANANA MILK SHAKE†

A pretty summer-time cooler.

½ cup fresh sliced strawberries
½ cup fresh sliced banana

¼ cup unsweetened apple juice
¼ cup unflavored yogurt

Combine all ingredients in a blender and blend until smooth. Pour into a tall glass and garnish with sliced strawberries. Serve chilled. Makes 10 ounces.

† Salt Free.

ORANGE MILK SHAKE†

Smooth and delicious.

1 cup unflavored yogurt
3 tablespoons orange juice concentrate,
   frozen

2 teaspoons honey

Chill the yogurt in the freezer for 1–2 hours before you intend to use it, then put all the ingredients in a blender and blend until well mixed. Serve at once. Makes 1 serving.

† Salt Free.

VANILLA MILK SHAKE†

Made with real ice cream, this is more of a dessert.

1 cup Vanilla Ice Cream (see index)
½ cup cold skim milk

¼ teaspoon vanilla

Mix in blender briefly then serve at once. Makes 1 serving.

† No Added Salt.

STRAWBERRY MILK SHAKE†

Follow the Vanilla Milk Shake recipe but use Strawberry Ice Cream and add ¼ cup frozen strawberries to the milk and blend. Serve at once. Makes 1 serving.

† No Added Salt.

CAROB MILK SHAKE†

Follow the Vanilla Milk Shake recipe but add 1 tablespoon sifted carob powder and 1 teaspoon honey to the milk and blend before adding the ice cream and vanilla. Serve at once. Makes 1 serving.

† No Added Salt.

HOT CAROB†

Children love this on cold mornings; adults do too!

2 teaspoons carob powder　　　　　　　　**1 cup milk**
1 teaspoon honey (or more to taste)

In a small sauce pan, mix the carob, honey and 1 tablespoon of the milk into a paste. Then gradually stir in the rest of the milk until well blended. Cook over low heat until hot. Do not boil. Serves 1.

† Salt Free.

INSTANT HOT CAROB†

Quick preparation and low in calories

2 teaspoons carob powder
⅓ cup nonfat instant milk

1 teaspoon honey (or more to taste)
1 cup (scant) hot water

In a glass or mug, mix together the carob and milk powder, then stir in the honey and hot water. Enjoy!

Note: For more protein, increase the instant milk to ½ or ⅔ cup.

† Salt Free.

EGGNOG†

A Christmas tradition.

1 cup milk
1 pint half and half
1 teaspoon vanilla

2 eggs, beaten until light and foamy
¼ cup honey
nutmeg

Mix all the ingredients except the nutmeg in the blender until smooth. Chill for several hours. Sprinkle with nutmeg before serving. Serves 4.

† Salt Free.

APPENDIX

Natural Food Distributors

BUTTE CREEK MILL   Box 561, Eagle Point, OR 97524
  Offers a variety of natural foods.
DIAMOND K ENTERPRISES   RR 1, Box 30, St. Charles, MN 55972
  Offers a variety of organic and natural foods.
GOLDEN ACRES, INC.   Lone Tree Way, Rt. 2, Box 207, Brentwood, CA 94513
  Sells fruits, nuts, spices, candies and seeds.
THE GREAT VALLEY MILLS   687 Mill Rd., Telford, PA 18969
  Offers a variety of natural foods.
JAFFE BROTHERS   P.O. Box 636, Valley Center, CA 92082–0636
  Offers a variety of organic and natural foods.
LAMB'S GRIST MILL   Rt. 1, Box 66, Hillsboro, TX 76645
  Sells stone ground corn meals.
MOORE'S FLOUR MILL   1605 Shasta St., Redding, CA 96001
  Offers a variety of organic and natural foods.
NEW HOPE MILLS   RFD #2, Box 269A, Moravia, NY 13118
  Sells flours, cornmeal, cereals and pancake mixes.
NICHOLS GARDEN NURSERY   1190 N. Pacific Hwy., Albany, OR 97321
  Sells, herbs, spices, milk cultures, oils and sourdough starter.
NORTHERN NATURAL FOODS   13 S. 4th St., Box 66, Moorhead, MN 56560
  Offers a variety of natural foods.
PAUL'S GRAINS   Rt. 1, Box 76, Laurel, IA 50141
  Offers a variety of organic and natural foods.
THE SCHOOL OF THE OZARKS   Point Lookout, MO 66726
  Sells stone ground flours, meals and mixes.
WALNUT ACRES   Penns Creeks, PA 17862
  Offers a variety of organic and natural foods.
WEST WIND FARM   Rt. 1, Box 67, Sheridan, OR 97378
  Sells organic grains and sprout seeds.
WOLFE'S NECK FARM   RR 1, Box 71, Freeport, ME 04032
  Sells frozen organic beef and lamb.

Recommended Reading

Let's Stay Healthy by Adelle Davis. Los Angeles, CA: Cancer Control Society, 1981.

Let's Have Healthy Children by Adelle Davis. New York: Harcourt Brace Jovanovich, Inc., 1972.

Diet For A Small Planet by Frances Moore Lappé. New York: Ballantine Books, 1971.

Live Longer Now by Jon N. Leonard et al. New York: Charter Books, 1981.

High Level Wellness by Donald B. Ardell. Emmaus, PA: Rodale Press, 1977.

Supermarket Handbook: Access to Whole Foods by Nikki and David Goldbeck. New York: Signet Books, 1976.

Old Fashioned Recipe Book: The Encyclopedia of Country Living by Carla Emery. New York: Bantam Books, 1977.

The Vegetarian Alternative by Vic Sussman. Emmaus, PA: Rodale Press, 1978.

Sugar Blues by William Duffy. New York: Warner Books, 1975.

The Practical Encyclopedia of Natural Healing by Mark Bricklin. Emmaus, PA: Rodale Press, 1976.

Sweet and Dangerous by John Yudkin, M.D. New York: Bantam Books.

Consumer Beware by Beatrice T. Hunter. New York: Simon and Schuster, 1972.

The Chemical Feast by James S. Turner. New York: Viking Press, 1970.

The Complete Book of Natural Foods by Fred Rohé. Boulder, CO: Shambhala Publications, Inc., 1983.

The Womanly Art of Breastfeeding by La Leche League International. Franklin Park, IL: La Leche League International, 1981.

Mothering Your Nursing Toddler by Norma Jane Bumgarner. Norman, OK: Norma Jane Bumgarner, 1980.

Garden Way's Guide to Food Dehydrating by Phyllis Hobson. Charlotte, VT: Garden Way Publishing, 1980.

The ABC's of Home Food Dehydration by Barbara Densley. Bountiful, UT: Horizon Publishers, 1975.

Dry and Save by Dora D. Flack. Salt Lake City, UT: Bookcraft, Inc., 1976.

Home Food Dehydrating by Jay and Shirley Bills. Bountiful, UT: Horizon Publishers, 1974.

The Encylopedia of Organic Gardening by the staff of Organic Gardening Magazine. Emmaus, PA: Rodale Press, 1978.

Gardening without Poisons by Beatrice T. Hunter. Los Angeles, CA: Regent House, 1980.

Organic Plant Protection by Roger B. Yepsen, Jr. Emmaus, PA: Rodale Press, 1976.

The Herb Book by John Lust. New York: Bantam Books, 1974.

Back to Eden by Jethro Kloss. Santa Barbara, CA: Woodbridge Press, 1975.

INDEX

Active dry yeast, 6, 9
Amino acids, 75
Apples
  Apple Banana Drink, 150
  Apple Crisp, 126
  Apple Nut Cake, 121
  Apple Pie, 116
  Baked Apples, 36
  Banapple Yogurt Milk Shake, 151
  Dried Apples, 66

Baked Apples, 36
Baked "French Fries", 52
Baked goods, storage of, 10
Bakeware, glass, 6
Baking, 9
Baking powder, aluminum-free, 6
Banana
  Banana Bread, 19
  Banana Carob Chip Cake, 121
  Banana-Coconut Cream Pie, 118
  Banana Nut Muffins, 20
  Banapple Yogurt Milk Shake, 151
  Dried Banana Slices, 67
  Frozen Bananas, 130
Barbequed Chicken, 89
Barbequed Spareribs, 89
Barley, unpearled, 4
Basic Pie Crust, 22
Beans
  Bean Burritos, 81
  Beans, basic, 83
  Bean Soup, 47
  Chili, 45
  Savory Bean Casserole, 97
Beef
  Beef Stroganoff, 97
  Goulash, 99
  Gyros, 99
  Oriental Liver, 96
  Potato Skillet Dinner, 98
  Risotto, 98
  Savory Bean Casserole, 97
  Sloppy Joes, 100
  Stir-Fried Pepper Steak, 95
  Toddler Meats, 102
Beverages
  description, 147
  Apple Banana Drink, 150
  Banapple Yogurt Milk Shake, 151
  Carob Milk Shake, 153
  Citrus Cooler, 150
  Eggnog, 154
  Herbal Tea, 148
  Hot Carob, 153
  Hot Russian Tea, 149
  Iced Tea, 148
  Instant Hot Carob, 154

Beverages (*Continued*)
  Melon Juice, 150
  Mulled Cider, 149
  Orange Milk Shake, 152
  Strawberry Banana Milk Shake, 151
  Strawberry Milk Shake, 153
  Tomato Juice, 151
  Tropical Delight, 150
  Vanilla Milk Shake, 152
Biscuits, 20
Blender, 6
Blintzes, 32
Blue Cheese Dip, 109
Blue Cheese Dressing, 55
Boston Brown Bread, 16
Bran, 4
Bran Muffins, 20
Bread, baking of, 9
Bread, quick
  Banana Bread, 19
  Banana Nut Muffins, 20
  Biscuits, 20
  Boston Brown Bread, 16
  Bran Muffins, 20
  Carrot Coconut Bread, 18
  Corn Bread, 17
  Gingerbread, 18
  Pumpkin Bread, 17
Bread, yeast
  Cinnamon Raisin Bread, 12
  Cinnamon Raisin Caramel Rolls, 12
  Cinnamon Raisin English Muffins, 14
  Cinnamon Raisin Whole Wheat Egg Bagels, 15
  English Muffins, 14
  Onion Bread, 13
  Onion Whole Wheat Egg Bagels, 15
  Pita Bread, 16
  Pumpernickel Bread, 13
  Whole Wheat Bread, 11
  Whole Wheat Egg Bagels, 15
  Whole Wheat Rolls, 13
Breakfast, 27
Brewer's yeast, 147
Broiled Fish, 100
Broiled Grapefruit, 35
Brownies, carob, 127
Brown rice, 4, 83
Butter, 5

Caffeine, 4, 115, 147, 148
Cake
  Apple Nut Cake, 121
  Banana Carob Chip Cake, 121
  Carob Cake, 122
  Carrot Cake, 123
Candy
  Caramels, 129
  Carob Halvah, 130

Candy (*Continued*)
  Carob Treat, 130
  Halvah, 129
  Super Fudge, 128
Caramels, 129
Carbohydrate, 4
Carob
  description, 4, 115
  Banana Carob Chip Cake, 121
  Carob Brownies, 127
  Carob Cake, 122
  Carob Chip Cookies, 137
  Carob Chip Ice Cream, 127
  Carob Delight, 110
  Carob Dessert Crêpes, 125
  Carob Fudge Sauce, 125
  Carob Halvah, 130
  Carob Milk Shake, 153
  Carob Peanut Butter Frosting, 122
  Carob-Peanut Butter Granola, 35
  Carob Pinwheels, 139
  Carob Treat, 130
  Double Carob Cheesecake, 120
  "Eagle" Bars, 142
  Frozen Bananas, 130
  Hot Carob, 153
  Instant Hot Carob, 154
  Super Fudge, 128
Carrots
  Carrot Cake, 123
  Carrot Coconut Bread, 18
  Dried Carrots, 65
  Steamed Sliced Carrots, 50
Cereal. *See also* Granola
  Cinnamon Raisin Oatmeal, 33
  Toddler Breakfasts, 40
Cheesecake
  Double Carob Cheesecake, 120
  Fresh Strawberry Cheesecake, 119
Cheese
  description, 5
  Cheese Crackers, 106
  Cheese Omelet, 28
  Cheesy Popcorn, 111
  Lasagna, 77
  Pizza, 78
  Potato Cheese Casserole, 80
  Quick Pizza, 79
  Vegetable Quiche, 76
Cherry Pie, 116
Chicken
  Barbequed Chicken, 89
  Chicken and Rice Bake, 88
  Chicken Noodle Soup, 46
  Chicken Pot Pie, 92
  Curried Chicken, 88
  Egg Rolls, 96
  Stir-Fried Chicken and Broccoli, 93
  Toddler Meats, 102
Chili, 45
Chocolate, 4, 115
Christmas Cookies, 138
Christmas Fruitcake, 124
Cinnamon Raisin Bread, 12
Cinnamon Raisin Caramel Rolls, 12
Cinnamon Raisin English Muffins, 14
Cinnamon Raisin Oatmeal, 33
Cinnamon Raisin Whole Wheat Egg Bagels, 15

Citrus Cooler, 150
Cocoa, 4
Coconut
  Banana-Coconut Cream Pie, 118
  Coconut Cream Pie, 117
  Coconut Macaroons, 139
  Coconut Pie Crust, 23
  Coconut Pudding, 118
  Strawberry Coconut Granola, 35
Complementary proteins, 75
Compote
  Spicy Fruit Compote, 38
  Sunny Fruit Compote, 38
Cookies
  description, 135
  baking, 135
  Carob Chip Cookies, 137
  Carob Pinwheels, 139
  Christmas Cookies, 138
  Coconut Macaroons, 139
  "Eagle" Bars, 142
  Fig Bars, 141
  Gingerbread Cookies, 140
  Oatmeal Raisin Cookies, 136
  Peanut Butter Cookies, 136
  Peanut Butter Balls, 143
  Strawberry Apple Bars, 143
  Three-In-One Cookie, 140
Cookware
  aluminum, 6
  cast iron, seasoning of, 6, 21
  glass, 6
  non-stick, 6
  stainless steel, 6
Corn
  Cornbread, 17
  cornmeal, 4
  Dried Corn, 66
  Steamed Corn, 50
Crackers
  description, 105
  Cheese Crackers, 106
  Graham Crackers, 107
  Rye Crackers, 107
  Sesame Crackers, 106
  Toddler Teething Crackers, 108
Cranberry Relish, 58
Cream Cheese Frosting, 124
Cream, Whipped, 128
Creamy Garlic Dressing, 56
Crêpes
  basic recipe, 21
  Carob Dessert Crêpes, 125
  Crêpes with Turkey in Velouté Sauce, 91
Crispy Baked Fish, 101
Croutons, 54
Cultured cottage cheese, 5

Dehydrator
  homemade, 61, 62
  manufactured, 6, 61, 62
Dip
  Blue Cheese Dip, 109
  Fresh Onion Dip, 108
  Fruit Dip, 109
Double Carob Cheesecake, 120
Dried Apples, 66

Dried Banana Slices, 67
Dried Carrots, 65
Dried Corn, 66
Dried foods, 43, 61–62
Dried fruit, 4, 61–62, 105, 135
Dried Herbs, 71
Dried Minced Onions, 64
Dried Mushrooms, 63
Dried Peaches, 67
Dried Pears, 68
Dried Pineapple Rings and Pieces, 68
Dried Potato Pieces, 64
Dried Tomato Slices, 63
Dried vegetables, 43, 61–62

"Eagle" Bars, 142
Eggs
    description, 5
    Cheese Omelet, 28
    Fruit Omelet, 28
    Omelet, 28
    Quiche, vegetable, 76
    Scrambled Eggs, 29
    Toddler Breakfasts, 40
Eggnog, 154
Egg Rolls, 96
English Muffins, 14

Fiber, 3, 4, 115
Fig Bars, 141
Fish
    Broiled Fish, 100
    Crispy Baked Fish, 101
    Fish Sandwich, 101
    Tuna Fish Hotdish, 102
Flour, texture of, 4, 9, 115, 135
Food labeling, 3
Food processor, 6
French Toast, 30. See also Toddler Breakfasts
Fresh Onion Dip, 108
Frosting
    Carob Peanut Butter Frosting, 122
    Cream Cheese Frosting, 124
Frozen Bananas, 130
Frozen desserts. See also Ice Cream
    Frozen Bananas, 130
    Pina Colada Yogurt Bars, 132
    Popsicles, 131
    Yogurt Bars, 131
    Yogurt Dream Bars, 132
Fructose, 4
Fruit
    fresh, 5, 61, 105
    frozen, 5
    Fruit and Nut Granola, 33
    Fruit Dip, 109
    Fruit Leather, 70
    Fruit Omelet, 28
    Summer Fruit Salad, 37
    Winter Fruit Salad, 37
Fruitcake. See Christmas Fruit Cake
Fruit Juice, 5, 147
Fudge
    Super Fudge, 128

Gardening, organic, 5, 43
Gingerbread, 18

Gingerbread Cookies, 140
Glucose, 4
Gluten, 4
Goulash, 99
Graham Crackers, 107
Grains, whole, 3, 4, 6, 27
Grain mill, 6
Granola
    Carob-Peanut Butter Granola, 35
    Fruit and Nut Granola, 33
    Maple Granola, 34
    Peanut Butter Granola, 34
    Strawberry Coconut Granola, 35
Grapefruit
    Broiled Grapefruit, 35
Gyros, 99

Halvah, 129
Hash Brown Potatoes, 52
Herb teas
    Herbal Tea, 148
    Hot Russian Tea, 149
    Iced Tea, 148
    Sun Tea, 148
Honey, 3, 4, 135
Hot Carob, 153

Ice Cream
    Carob Chip Ice Cream, 127
    Strawberry Ice Cream, 128
    Vanilla Ice Cream, 127
Ice cream maker, 6
Iced Tea, 148
Instant Blintz, 32
Iron, 4, 18, 147
Italian Dressing, 54

Kibbutz Breakfast, 39
Kneading, 9

Lacto-ovo vegetarian, 75
Lasagna, 77
Legumes, 75
Lentils, 5, 75
Lentil Vegetable Soup, 48

Macaroni and Cheese, 78
Maple Granola, 34
Maple Syrup, 4
Mayonnaise, 55
Meat, 5, 75, 87
Melon Juice, 150
Middle Eastern flatbread, 16
Milk, non-fat powder, 5, 11
Milk shake
    Banapple Yogurt Milk Shake, 151
    Carob Milk Shake, 153
    Orange Milk Shake, 152
    Strawberry Banana Milk Shake, 151
    Strawberry Milk Shake, 153
    Vanilla Milk Shake, 152
Milk, skim, 5, 147
Molasses, 4, 16, 147
Monosodium glutamate, 6
Mulled Cider, 149

Mushrooms
    Dried Mushrooms, 63
    Steamed Whole Mushrooms, 50

Natural foods, 3–6, 27, 105, 115, 147
Natural Food Coloring, 138
Nitrate, 5, 87
Noodles. *See* Whole Wheat Noodles
Nuts, 3, 5, 105, 135

Oatmeal, Cinnamon Raisin Oatmeal, 33
Oatmeal Raisin Cookies, 136
Oil, unrefined varieties, 5
Omelet, 28
Onions
    Dried Minced Onions, 64
    Onion Bread, 13
    Onion Whole Wheat Egg Bagels, 15
Orange Milk Shake, 152
Orange Coconut Coffee Cake, 31
Organically grown, 5, 43
Oriental Liver, 96
Oven drying, 61, 62

Pancakes, 30
Pancake syrup, 4
Pasta maker, 6
Pastry flour, 4, 115, 135
Peanut butter
    description, 3, 5, 105
    Carob Peanut Butter Frosting, 122
    Carob-Peanut Butter Granola, 35
    Peanut Butter Balls, 143
    Peanut Butter Cookies, 136
    Peanut Butter Granola, 34
Pete's Pickles, 57
Pickles, garlic dill
    Pete's Pickles, 57
Pie
    Apple Pie, 116
    Banana-Coconut Cream Pie, 118
    Coconut Cream Pie, 117
    Fresh Cherry Pie, 116
    Pumpkin Pie, 117
Pie crust
    Basic Pie Crust, 22
    Coconut Pie Crust, 23
    Tomato Rye Pie Crust, 23
Pina Colada Yogurt Bars, 132
Pita Bread, 16
Pizza, 78
Pocket bread, 16
Popcorn
    Cheesy Popcorn, 111
    snack, 6
Popcorn popper, hot air, 6
Popsicles, 131
Pork
    Barbequed Spareribs, 89
    Egg Rolls, 96
    Sweet and Sour Pork, 94
    Toddler Meats, 102
Potatoes
    Baked "French Fries", 52
    Dried Potato Pieces, 64
    Hash Brown Potatoes, 52

Potatoes (*Continued*)
    Potato Cheese Casserole, 80
    Potato Skillet Dinner, 98
    Steamed Sliced Potatoes, 50
Protein, sources of, 5, 27, 75, 105, 135
Pudding, Coconut, 118
Pumpernickel Bread, 13
Pumpkin Bread, 17
Pumpkin Pie, 117

Quick Pizza, 79

Reconstitution, dried foods, 62
Rice
    description, 4
    Chicken and Rice Bake, 88
    Rice, 83
    Risotto, 98
    Stuffed Peppers, 77
Rice flour, 4, 17
Risotto, 98
Roast Turkey, 90
Rolled oats, 4
Rye
    flour, 4
    Pumpernickel Bread, 13
    Rye Crackers, 107
    Tomato Rye Pie Crust, 23

Salad, 53
Salad Dressing
    Blue Cheese Dressing, 55
    Creamy Garlic Dressing, 56
    Italian Dressing, 54
    Mayonnaise, 55
    Vinaigrette Dressing, 54
Salt, 3, 6, 105
Salt free. *See* Table of Contents
Salt, not added. *See* Table of Contents
Sandwiches, 84
Savory Bean Casserole, 97
Scotch Shortbread, 141
Scrambled Eggs, 29
Sea salt, 6
Sesame Crackers, 106
Sloppy Joes, 100
Snacks. *See also* Crackers
    description, 105
    Carob Delight, 110
    Cheesy Popcorn, 111
    dried fruit, 4, 61–62, 105
    Fruit Leather, 70
    Sunflower Seed Snack, 111
    Trail Mix, 109
Soups
    Bean Soup, 47
    Chicken Noodle Soup, 46
    Chili, 45
    Lentil Vegetable Soup, 48
    Turkey Barley Soup, 49
    Turkey Vegetable Soup, 44
Spicy Fruit Compote, 38
Steamed Vegetables, 50
Stir-Fried Chicken and Broccoli, 93
Stir-Fried Pepper Steak, 95
Stir-Fried Vegetables, 51

Strawberry
  Fresh Strawberry Cheesecake, 119
  Strawberry Apple Bars, 143
  Strawberry Banana Milk Shake, 151
  Strawberry Coconut Granola, 35
  Strawberry Ice Cream, 128
  Strawberry Milk Shake, 153
Stuffed Peppers, 77
Sucrose, 4
Sugar, 3, 4, 115
Summer Fruit Salad, 37
Sun drying, 61, 62
Sunflower Seed Snack, 111
Sunny Fruit Compote, 38
Sun Tea, 148
Super Fudge, 128
Sweet and Sour Pork, 94

Tamari, 6
Tartar Sauce, 56
Tea
  Herbal Tea, 148
  Hot Russian Tea, 149
  Iced Tea, 148
  Sun Tea, 148
Three-In-One Cookie, 140
Toddler Breakfasts, 40
Toddler Meats, 102
Toddler Teething Crackers, 108
Toddler teething food, 67, 108
Toddler Vegetables, 51
Tomato
  Chili, 45
  Dried Tomato Slices, 63
  Steamed, Sliced Tomato, 50
  Tomato Juice, 151
  Tomato Rye Pie Crust, 23
  Tomato Sauce, 57
  Vegetable Quiche, 76
  Vegetarian Stew, 82
Tortillas, 21
Trail Mix, 109
Tropical Delight, 150
Tuna Fish Hotdish, 102
Turkey
  Crêpes with Turkey in Velouté Sauce, 91
  Roast Turkey, 90
  Turkey Barley Soup, 49
  Turkey Pot Pie, 92
  Turkey Vegetable Soup, 44

Undyed cheese, 5
Unfiltered fruit juice, 5, 147

Vanilla Ice Cream, 127
Vanilla Milk Shake, 152
Vegetable
  fresh, 5, 43, 61, 62
  frozen, 5, 43
  Lentil Vegetable Soup, 48
  Steamed Vegetables, 50
  Stir-Fried Vegetables, 51
  Toddler Vegetables, 51
  Turkey Vegetable Soup, 44
  Vegetable Quiche, 76
  Vegetarian Stew, 82
Vegetable oils, 5
Vegetable steamer, 6, 50, 51
Vegetarian
  description, 75
  Beans, 83
  Bean Burritos, 81
  Lasagna, 77
  Macaroni and Cheese, 78
  Pizza, 78
  Potato Cheese Casserole, 80
  Quick Pizza, 79
  Rice, 83
  Sandwiches, 84
  Stuffed Peppers, 77
  Vegetable Quiche, 76
  Vegetarian Stew, 82
Vinaigrette Dressing, 54

Whipped Cream, 128
Whole foods, storage of, 3
Wheat germ, 3, 4
Whole grains
  description, 3, 4, 6
  storage of, 3
Whole Wheat Bread, 11
Whole Wheat Egg Bagels, 15
Whole wheat flour, 3, 4, 9, 115
Whole Wheat Noodles, 22
Whole Wheat Rolls, 13
Winter Fruit Salad, 37

Yeast bread. *See* Bread, yeast
Yogurt
  description, 5
  Banapple Yogurt Milk Shake, 151
  Pina Colada Yogurt Bars, 132
  Yogurt, 39
  Yogurt Bars, 131
  Yogurt Dream Bars, 132
Yogurt maker, 6

ABOUT THE AUTHOR

Victoria P. Cavalier has been teaching natural food cooking since 1978, combining her personal experience, research and experimentation with her love of cooking fine foods. She has a B.S. in commercial art and journalism and had her first freelance article published in a major magazine in 1973. Since then her work has appeared in a variety of magazines and her art has been shown in galleries and private collections throughout the United States. She has also worked as a newspaper reporter and photographer in Ohio and West Virginia.

An advocate of not only natural foods, but a natural lifestyle, Victoria's other pursuits include organic gardening, spinning natural fibers, weaving, sewing, hiking, running, cross county skiing, horseback riding, environmental issues, and "natural mothering."